1514.   CRM

£ 2.99

8/50

ESSENTIAL WORDS

*A Basic Vocabulary of New Testament Greek
with Notes*

David Finnemore Hill

MINERVA PRESS
ATLANTA LONDON SYDNEY

ISBN 0 75410 640 3

First Published 1999 by
MINERVA PRESS
315–317 Regent Street
London W1R 7YB

Printed in Great Britain for Minerva Press

ESSENTIAL WORDS
A Basic Vocabulary of New Testament Greek with Notes

By the same author

An Archer Looks at the Bible, Pentland Press
(Foreword by Robert Hardy)

To the memory of the late

Agnes S. Paul, M.A., B.D.
John A. Mandall, M.A.
Roy McIntyre Smith, M.A., LL.B.

Note on the Cover

The figures on the cover of a man (or an angel), a lion, an ox, and an eagle go to back to Ezekiel 1 (early in the sixth century BC) and were repeated in Revelation 4. The identification with the four evangelists was due to St Jerome (c. AD 345–420).

The illumination comes from the *Book of Kells*, Co. Meath (c. AD 800). The author is grateful to Trinity College, Dublin for permission to reproduce the image and to the Bishop of Oxford for his suggestion of the illustration.

About the Author

This vocabulary must have had the longest gestation period in textbook history, for Dr David Finnemore Hill, who is now retired, began it two years before going up to St John's College, Durham. Here he read Theology and Greek as part of a general degree, later following it up with an M.A. Later still, in his thirties, he read for his Ph.D. in the Department of Greek at the University of Leeds. He runs a Greek Testament Group, which he initiated in 1983, in the Diocese of Guildford, and attempted to encourage groups in a score of other dioceses. He co-edited his church's parish magazine for seventeen years.

His working life was chiefly spent on teaching Scripture and Latin at Dane Court School, near Woking, with English and General Knowledge as subsidiary subjects.

Dr Hill was an officer of the Durham University Society for twenty-six years and still serves on two committees. He sits on Convocation Committee at Leeds and was two years on Court at the University.

He has been involved with the bow over many years and coaches at a local school, being Past President of The Association for Archery in Schools. He is currently President of The Society of Archer-Antiquaries and was for three years Gentleman Vice-President of The County of Surrey Archery Association.

He and his wife have two daughters in their twenties.

Acknowledgements

I am grateful to the late Rev. Professor G.D. Kilpatrick, D.D., of The Queen's College, Oxford, for general guidance and encouragement; to the late Rev. C.R.P. Anstey, formerly, Vice-Principal of Chichester Theological College, and The Rev. Brian Coleman, Vicar of All Saints', Guildford for particular assistance; to The Rev. Robert Morgan and The Rev. Richard Smail at Oxford for their comments; and for their patience to my early tutors, in whose memory the textbook is affectionately dedicated.

Foreword

Once, when I was principal of a theological college, I wrote to a well-known bishop asking his permission to exempt one particular ordinand from further study of New Testament Greek. The bishop replied (I still have his letter): 'I studied New Testament Greek myself, gained one hundred per cent in the examination and received a telegram of congratulation from the examiner! But I cannot recall one instance in my long pastoral ministry when it has been of the slightest use to me!'

Many years earlier, I was at another theological college. An old clergyman from Lincolnshire indicated that he would dearly love to come and speak to the students, to give a devotional address at Compline, the late evening service. I still remember his opening sentence: 'My brethren, I do beseech you not to read too many books. There is only one book – the *Novum Testamentum Graece*.'

I am convinced that both the prelate and the priest were *wrong*. But I have more sympathy with the latter!

Dr David Finnemore Hill has performed a very valuable service and filled an important gap by providing this book of essential words from the Greek New Testament. It's a kind of 'Greek without Tears', and will, I believe, be especially useful to those coming new to the study of the language. This includes those beginning to read for theology degrees and diplomas, ordinands in theological colleges, and indeed anyone who discovers an interest in the books of the New Testament as they were originally written. The emphasis, quite rightly, is upon the words *in their context* (hence the passages suggested for translation). Dr Hill is also intrigued, as I am, by the derivations of words and he communicates that fascination.

The work must have demanded hours of painstaking labour, but there is no doubt that it has been a labour of love. Those who have been regular or even occasional members of the Greek Testament Group, which has been going since 1983 and which he started, in the Diocese of Guildford, can hardly fail to have been affected by Dr Hill's enthusiasm for the language and for an informed understanding of the text of the Gospels and Epistles in particular.

I have little doubt that those who use *Essential Words* as a tool, and persist, even when the going gets more difficult (as it is bound to do with the study of any language) will find themselves caught up into this love of the words of the Greek New Testament. And if you get no further than Part One (which would be a pity), you would still be well acquainted with the first one hundred basic words of vocabulary with their definitions and their setting in Greek sentences. And that's enough to start with and to feel much less daunted not only by the New Testament in its original tongue but also by many scholarly books about it, which tend to be bespattered with Greek words.

'Can we rescue a word, and discover a universe? Can we study a language, and awake to the Truth? Can we bury ourselves in a lexicon, and arise in the presence of God?' So asked Sir Edwyn Hoskyns in his *Cambridge Sermons*.

I believe we can. Let's find out.

David P. Wilcox
formerly Bishop of Dorking
and Principal of Ripon College, Cuddesdon

Preface

There are some 5,500 different Greek words in the New Testament; over half of them only occur three times or less. About 1,600 are just found once – 29% of the total. Nothing could demonstrate more clearly and concisely the need of a basic vocabulary to ensure that the beginner makes the best use of his time and energy, and that the more advanced student knows the important words to revise. Perhaps it resembles C.K. Ogden's Basic English of 850 words, compiled in the 1920s, to which 150 were added for the New Testament version.

About 700 words – approximately an eighth of the total as it happens – have been carefully selected and arranged in three parts. The first consists of the hundred most frequent ones in six sections, with thirty-six made-up sentences for practice on these words. This has been done in order not to overload the word lists of the early reading texts. The learner is asked to translate these Greek sentences as practice, but English answers are given.

The second part contains some 440 new words, illustrated by passages from the Gospels and Acts. The final part consists of 170 words found more often in the Epistles, and will be demonstrated where possible by extracts from them. In addition, in each section of parts two and three there are notes to help the beginner. It may be added that this scheme of reading texts is not new, but has been used in popular works both on classical and on modern Greek. Students need, of course, to obtain their own Greek

Testaments and grammars, since the text itself is not provided here.

The definitions in the Special Vocabularies for each section have been kept as simple and short as possible. For fuller explanations and for revision, reference should always be made to the General Vocabulary at the back. It is suggested that the student revises words in groups of ten or by taking a letter of the alphabet at a time where this is convenient.

The book will be of occasional use and interest to the classical scholar, who turns later to the study of the language of the New Testament. It is, however, primarily intended for those coming quite new to Greek, perhaps long after they have left school, such as those working for the General Ordination Examination and the Free Church equivalents, students on university degree or diploma courses, and especially those on the Lambeth Diploma or S. Th. syllabus.

Suggested links to
J.W. Wenham, *The Elements of New Testament Greek*

Regarding Part One, it is recommended that Section 1 is learnt when Exercise 5 in Wenham is reached. The other five sections can be done in parallel, so that Section 6 is arrived at with Exercise 10.

It is suggested that the texts in Part Two are studied again in parallel with the chapters in Wenham, beginning with Exercise number 11. This leaves a dozen sections over, after Wenham is completed, and as the words are introduced at different times, any further co-ordination would not seem possible.

Part Three should not be attempted, perhaps, until Wenham is finished, for the latter has only some 60 of the 170 words in the Epistle vocabulary.

Contents

Abbreviations

abs.	absolutely (without an object)	imp.	imperative
		imperf.	imperfect tense
acc.	accusative	impers.	impersonal
act.	active voice	ind.	indirect (-ly)
adj.	adjective	indef.	indefinite
adv.	adverb	indic.	indicative
aor.	aorist tense	infin.	infinitive
art.	article	intr.	intransitive
cf.	compare (sometimes used where derivations are indirect – e.g., via Latin)	interrog.	interrogative
		κτλ	και τα λοιπα and the remainder
		lit.	literal (-ly)
comp.	comparative	Lucan	characteristic of the Third Gospel and/or Acts
contr.	contracted		
dat.	dative	LXX	Septuagint
dist.	distinguish	m.	masculine
esp.	especially	Marcan	characteristic of Mark's Gospel
f.	feminine		
fig.	figurative (-ly)	Matthaean	characteristic of the First Gospel
fut.	future tense	mid.	middle voice
gen.	genitive/generally	n.	neuter
gen.	genitive absolute	neg.	negative

abs.			
GV	General Vocabulary	nom.	nominative
NT	New Testament	plup.	pluperfect tense
obj.	object	p.p.s	principal parts of verbs
		pron.	pronoun
opt.	optative mood	rel.	relative
OT	Old Testament	s.	singular
part.	participle/particle	subj.	subjunctive/subject
pass.	passive voice	tr.	transitive
perf.	perfect tense	vb.	verb
pl.	plural	voc.	vocative
		w.	with

±	plus or minus (with or without)
=	agreeing with
≡	equivalent to

A comma divides synonyms, such as 'whole, all'.
A semi-colon divides different nuances or meanings for the same word, such as 'I am astonished; I am mad', 'I carry; I endure', 'honour; price'.

PART ONE
A Hundred Basic Basics

Introduction

In this part the hundred most common words are given, together with phrases and sentences for elementary practice.

For fuller definitions and for revision, reference should always be made to the General Vocabulary at the back of the book.

Section 1

ὁ, ἡ, το (m., f., n.)	the (see GV for uses)
πιστευω	I believe (often w. dat.), I trust in/on
ἀνθρωπος (Lat. *homo*)	a human being, man [*anthropology*]
φοβεομαι	I fear; I reverence [*phobia*]
ὀνομα, -ατος, το	name [*onomatopoeia*]
ἀκουω (l aor. ἠκουσα)	I hear, listen (often w. gen.) [*acoustics*]
ἀδελφος	brother (in wide sense) [*Philadelphia*]
πνευμα, -ατος, το	wind, breath; spirit [*pneumatic*] (see GV for five distinct uses)
εἰμι, ἐσομαι (fut.), ἠν (imp.)	I am, exist (see GV)
δυναμις, -εως, ἡ	power, ability; (pl.) powerful works [*dynamic*]
μετα (prep. w. gen.) (w. acc.)	with, in company with after (mostly re time) [*metaphysics*]
φωνη	a sound; voice [*telephone*]
ἀνηρ, ἀνδρος, ὁ (Lat. *vir*)	a man, a husband [*polyandry*]
γραφω	I write [*telegraph*]
πολυς, πολλη, πολυ	much, many; long (time) [*polytheism*]

24

λογος   word; saying; speech (see GV)
                         [*philology*]

Translate

1. πιστευε τω ἀνθρωπω.
2. φοβουμεθα το ὀνομα.
3. ἠκουον των ἀδελφων πολλα.
4. το Πνευμα ἐστι δυναμις.
5. μετα την φωνην ἐφοβουμην.
6. μετα των ἀνδρων ἐσεται.
7. γραψετε πολλους λογους.

Answers on pages 40

Section 2

ὅς, ἥ, ὅ (m., f., n.) definite
relative pron.

who, which, what, that
(see GV)

περι (prep. w. gen. mostly)

concerning, about;
on account of;

    (w. acc., local and
    occasionally temporal)

around, about
[*perimeter* re space;
perinatal re time]

γυνη, γυναικος, ἡ
(voc. γυναι
dat. pl. γυναιξι)

a woman, wife [*gynaecology*]

λαλεω

I speak, say (more dignified
than classical 'chatter') [*glossolalia*]

οὑτος, αὑτη, τουτο
(demonstrative adj. and pron.)

this; he, she, it, they

γραμματευς, -εως

scribe, teacher of the Law

φως, φωτος, το

light [*photography*]

οὑδεις, οὑδεμια, οὑδεν
[Lat. *nemo, nihil*]

(noun) no one, nothing
(adj.) no [Lat. *nullus*]

γινωσκω

I am taking in knowledge,
perceive;
(past tenses) I know, realise

προφητης, -ου

a prophet (see GV)

μαθητης, -ου

a learner, disciple
[*mathematics*]

ὑπο (prep. w. gen.)
    (w. acc.)

by (direct agent)
under [*hypodermic*]

λαος

a people; the crowd [*laity*]

κυριος	owner, master; Sir! (the) Lord (see GV)
ὑμεις, ὑμας, ὑμων, ὑμιν	you (pl.)
συ	you (s.)
εἰς (prep. w. acc.)	(place) into, towards; [eisegesis] (time) for, until;
εἰς το + infin.	for purpose, result κ.τ.λ. (see GV)
πολις, -εως, ἡ	a city [political]
ἀποστελλω (1 aor. -εστειλα)	I send away, commission [apostolic]

Translate

8. γραφεις ὅ ἀκουεις.

9. περι της γυναικος λαλησουσι.

10. οὑτοι οἱ γραμματεις φοβουνται το φως.

11. οὐδεις γινωσκει το ὀνομα του προφητου.

12. οἱ μαθηται ὑπο του λαου ἐπιστευοντο.

13. ὁ Κυριος ὑμας εἰς την πολιν ἀποστελλει.

Answers on page 40

Section 3

σωμα, -ατος, το — the body (alive or dead) (see GV) [*psychosomatic*]

ἡμεις, ἡμας, ἡμων, ἡμιν — we, us (declined pl. of ἐγω, I) (the nom. for emphasis or contrast)

ἐχω (2 aor. ἐσχον) — I have, hold, possess (see GV)

πορευομαι — I journey, proceed, go (also fig.)

δυο (dat. δυσι) — two (cf. Lat., *dual*)

ἡμερα — day; 'twenty-four hours'; Last Day; time in general [*ephemeral*]

πατηρ, πατρος, ὁ — father; male ancestor; God the Father (cf. Lat., *paternal*)

υἱος — a son (lit. and fig.)

φερω (2 aor. ἠνεγκον) — (cf. Lat.: *fero, tuli, latum*) I carry, bear; I bring (a common defective verb, in which other tenses are supplied by different roots – cf. English 'go' and 'went')

ἐγω, ἐμε, ἐμου, ἐμοι (or simply με, κ.τ.λ.) — I, me, of me, to/for me (nom. for emphasis or contrast) [*egocentric*]

28

ἐπι (prep. w. acc. most often) (place) on, upon, over
(lit and fig., and frequently
after verbs of motion);
[*epidermis*]
(time) during, as long as
(For uses w. gen. and dat.,
see GV)

γη the earth, soil, land
[*geology*]

τιθημι (1 aor. ἐθηκα) I put, place, set forth;
I appoint
[*antithesis, synthetic*]

οὐν so, therefore, then

χειρ, -ος, ἡ (dat. pl. χερσι) hand [*chiropodist*]

νυν, νυνι now (sometimes w. prep.);
the present (w. article)

δυναμαι I am powerful, able;
    (w. infin.) I am able to, I can
[*dynasty*]

λαμβανω (2 aor. ἐλαβον) I take, lay hold of;
I receive, get
(*epilepsy*)

συ, σε, σου, σοι you, you, of you,
    (2nd pers. s. declined) to/for you
(the nom. for emphasis or contrast)

Translate

14. τα σωματα ἡμων ἐχει ὀνοματα (note: sing. vb. w. n. pl. subject).

15. Προφητα, πορευσεις περι την πολιν δυο ἡμερας;

16. οἱ πατερες τους υἱους φερουσι.

17. ἐγω το σωμα ἐπι την γην ἐθηκα.

18. ὁ οὐν ἀνηρ τη χειρι ἐγραψε.

19. νυν δυναμεθα λαβειν σε.

Answers on pages 40–41

Section 4

πας, πασα, παν
(παντος gen., m. and n.)

(sing.)	every, the whole, all the…;
(pl.)	all, all the… (see GV)
	[*panorama*]

και — and, also; even

θεος — God (± article); a god, deity
[*theophany*]

ευρισκω (2 aor. ευρον) — I find; I find out, discover;
I find for myself, obtain
[*heuristic*]

εκεινος, -η, -ο — (demon. pron.) he, she, it, they
(implying remoteness)

(adj.) — that, those

εν (w. dat.) — in (place, time, κ. τ. λ. – see GV)
[*enthusiast*]

συν (w. dat.) — with, in company with
(less frequent than
μετα – see GV)
[*syntax; synthetic*]

τις (m. and f.), τι (n.), τινος (indef. pron.) someone, anyone
something, anything;
(adj.) a certain, some (dist. fr.
τίς;)

ερχομαι (2 aor. ηλθον) — I come; (rarely) I go (see GV for
p.p.s)

προς (w. acc.)	to, towards (of persons, places, things; w. vbs. of motion and saying) (See GV for several other uses)
οὐ	(οὐκ before smooth breathings; οὐχ before rough) not;
οὐ (interjection)	No! [*Utopia – 'no place'*] It is generally employed w. indic. and for a denial of fact – see μη. In questions, it expects the answer Yes (Lat. *nonne*)
θελω, ἐθελω (1 aor. ἠθελησα)	I am willing, I wish (w. infin., obj. or subjunctive)
ἰδιος, -α, -ον	one's own, private, personal [*idiom*; *idiot*]
ἀλλά	but (± a previous negation) (dist. fr. ἄλλα other things)
διδωμι (1 aor. ἐδωκα)	I give (in numerous senses; for p.p.s, see GV) [*antidote*]
αὐτος, -η, -ο	(emphatic pron.)self; he, she, it, they [*automatic*] (in gen.) his, her, its, their
τίς; (m. and f.), τί; (n.), τίνος; (interrog. pron. and adj.)	who? which? what?; why? (dist. from non-interrog. τις)
γαρ	for (main meaning; second word in a clause)
ποιεω	I make, produce; I do, perform [*poet*]

τε	and;
τε... και, τε και, τε... τε	both... and (second word in clause; see GV)

Translate

20. παντες οἱ ἀνθρωποι ἠκουσαν των προφητων και τον Θεον εὑρον.

21. ἐκεινοι οἱ ἀδελφοι ἠσαν ἐν τη πολει συν τῳ πατρι.

22. υἱος τις ἠλθε προς μητερα τινα.

23. οὐ θελεις εὑρειν τα ἰδια;

24. ἀλλα ὁ Κυριος ἐδωκε δυναμιν τοις μαθηταις αὐτου.

25. τίς γαρ πεποιηκε τους τε ἀνθρωπους και τας γυναικας;

Answers on page 41

Section 5

τοτε

then, at that time; thereupon
(Matthaean favourite)

ὁραω (2 aor. εἶδον)
    (in prohibitions)

I see; I perceive, discern;
see... do not, beware lest...
(Another common defective verb,
in which other tenses are supplied
by different roots – see GV for
p.p.s) [*panorama*]

ἐκ, ἐξ (prep. w. gen.)

from out of, from (place, time,
origin – see GV) [*exodus; ecstasy*]

μεν

a generally untranslatable
particle, usually answered by δε
or other conjunction, each of
the two introducing a clause to
be contrasted with the other.
See Matt. 3:11.

λεγω (2 aor. εἶπον)

I say, speak (including thought
and writing)
(For p.p.s of this common
defective verb, and for numerous
other meanings, see GV)

δε

but, on the other hand; and (a
weak adversative particle, generally
placed second in its clause, and
often answering μεν)

ἰδε, ἰδου

see! lo! (see GV for difference)

γινομαι (2 aor. mid. ἐγενομην)	I come into being (persons, things, occurrences); I happen (events); I am made; I become
φημι (2 aor. ἐφην)	I say (often in quoting or inter- jecting)
εἰ	if (introducing clauses w. indic.);
εἰ μη	if not, unless, except; if, whether (in indirect and direct questions); indeed, assuredly (not) (in strong statements, oaths etc.)
ἀν	an untranslatable conditional particle – 'in that case', 'any- how'. Its general effect is to make a statement *contingent*, which would otherwise be definitive. (See GV)
ὁτι	because; that (introducing noun clauses after verbs of saying, thinking, knowing, seeing, feeling)
εἱς, μια, ἑν (ἑνος m. and n. gen.)	one [*henotheism*]
ἡ	or (between words or sentences); than (in comparative sentences, w. same case after as before; the alter- native construction to 'genitive of comparison')

35

οὔτως	so, thus, in this way
ἑως (conjunction)	until (w. indic. for definite past time; w. aor. subj. for indefinite time) (See GV)
(preposition w. nouns in genitive, advbs. or other preps.)	
(time)	until, up to;
(place)	as for as, up to;
(measure)	as much as
ἀποκρινομαι (1 aor. pass. ἀπεκριθην)	I answer, reply (often used redundantly); I begin to speak

Translate

26. τοτε εἰδομεν αὐτην ἐκπορευομενην ἐκ της πολεως.

27. αἱ μεν γυναικες ἐλεγον· οἱ δε ἀνδρες τα σωματα ἡνεγκον.

28. ἰδε, ὁ ἀνηρ θεος γινεται, ἐφη.

29. οὗτος, εἰ ἠν προφητης, ἐγινωσκεν ἀν ταυτην, ὁτι μαθητης ἐστι.

30. εἰς ἡ δυο προφηται οὔτως εἰπον.

31. ἐαν ἐλθῃ ἑως της πολεως, τοις ἀδελφοις ἀποκρινειται.

Answers on page 41

Section 6

μη

Not. Used where something is indefinite or hypothetical, as opposed to οὐ the negative of fact. Normally οὐ negates the indicative; μη, the other moods – usually including participles. For four other uses, see GV

δια (prep. w. gen.)

through; throughout; by (place, time, means); [*diathermy*]

(w. acc.)

on account of, by reason of (see GV for compounds)

ἑαυτου, -ης, -ου

(reflexive pronoun)
self, selves (for almost all persons and genders, s. and pl., according to context)

ἐρωταω, ἐπερωταω

I ask a question, I question;
I request, beg (= αἰτεω)

ἱστημι *transitive*

in pres., imp., fut., and 1 aor. act. (ἐστησα) and in pass.
I make to stand, establish, set up;

intransitive

in perf., plup. (w. sense of pres. and imp.) and in 2 aor. act. (ἐστην)
I am set up, I stand
(see GV for p.p.s)

παρα (prep. w. acc.)	beside; against; more than [*paradox*]
(w. gen.)	from beside (chiefly w. companions, possessions etc.)
(w. dat.)	beside, in house of (almost always w. persons) [*paragraph*] (see GV)
ἱνα (conj.)	in order that…, so that… (see GV for six distinct uses)
ἱνα μη	that… not, lest
κατα (prep. w. gen.)	against, down from, throughout; [*catastrophe*]
(w. acc.)	according to (more often w. acc. and w. numerous meanings. See GV)
οἱδα	I know (a fact);
(w. infin.)	I know how to…; I know (a person, esp. God)
ὡς (adv.)	as (ὡς… οὑτως or v.v.: as… so, so… as; w. nom., acc., prep., verb, part. or gen. abs.); about (before numbers); how (before adjs. and advbs.)
(conj.)	temporal: as, when, since; while, when, as long as; (final) in order that, to…
(w. infin.)	
ἁπο (prep. w. gen.)	from, away from; by (expressing agent = ὑπο) (see GV for multiple uses) [*apostasy*]

Translate

32. μη φοβου, δια το φως.

33. ἐαυτον ἐρωτησει πολλα.

34. ὁ υἱος ἐστη παρα τῳ πατρι.

35. οἱ γραμματεις εἰπον ἱνα στησωσι τον λαον κατα τον λογον του Θεου.

36. οἰδαμεν ὁτι ἐπορευσατο δια της πολεως ὡς εὑρειν τα ἰδια ὁτι ἀπο σου ἡκουσαμεν.

Answers on pages 42–42

Answers to Exercises

Section 1

1.   Believe (you, s.) the man!

2.   We fear the name.

3.   They (or I) used to hear the brothers frequently.

4.   The Spirit is power.

5.   After the sound, I was afraid.

6.   He will be with the men.

7.   You will write many words.

Section 2

8.   You write what you hear.

9.   They will talk about the woman.

10.   These scribes fear the light.

11.   Nobody is getting to know the name of the prophet.

12.   The disciples were believed by the people.

13.   The Lord is sending you into the city.

Section 3

14.   Our bodies have names.

15.   Will you go around the city for two days, Prophet?

16.   The fathers are carrying the sons.

17.   *I* placed the body upon the ground.

18. So the man wrote with his hand.

19. We can now take you.

Section 4

20. All the men listened to the prophets and found God.

21. Those brothers were in the city with (their) father.

22. Any son came towards some mother (i.e., as in a party game).

23. Don't you want to find your own things?

24. But the Lord gave power to His disciples.

25. For who has made both men and women?

Section 5

26. We saw her coming out of the city at that time.

27. The women kept talking, but the men carried the corpses.

28. 'Look – the man is becoming a god,' he said.

29. This fellow, if he were a prophet, would know this woman because she is a disciple.

30. One or two prophets spoke as follows…

31. If he does come as far as the city, he will answer the brothers.

Section 6

32. Don't be afraid because of the light.

33. He will ask himself many things.

34. The son stood beside his father.

35. The scribes spoke in order that they might set up the people according to the word of God.

36. We know that he went through the city to find his belongings because we heard from you.

PART TWO
440 words characteristic of the Gospels and Acts

1. Peter Walks on the Water
   (Matthew 14:28–33)

Basic Words

ὑδωρ, ὑδατος, το	water [*hydrant*]
καταβαινω (2 aor. -εβην)	I descend, disembark (irregular aor. part. here)
πλοιον	boat, ship
περιπατεω	I walk [*peripatetic*]
βλεπω	I see, look at
ἀνεμος	wind [*anemometer*]
ἀρχομαι (1 aor. ἠρξαμην)	I begin
κραζω (1 aor. ἐκραξα)	I shout, cry out
σῳζω (1 aor. ἐσωσα)	I save, rescue
εὐθεως, εὐθυς	immediately, at once (sometimes weakened to an inferential 'then', 'so then': e.g., in Mark 1)
ἐπιλαμβανομαι	I take hold of
ἀναβαινω (2 aor. ἀνεβην)	I go up, ascend
προσκυνεω	I worship, do obeisance to
ἀληθως	truly, indeed

General Notes

28.	ἀποκριθεις	1 aor. part. 'having answered' (often redundant)
28.	κελευσον κελευω	1 aor. imper. I order, command
28.	ἐλθειν	2 aor. infin. ἐρχομαι
29.	ἐλθε	2 aor. imper. ἐρχομαι
29.	ἠλθεν	2 aor. indic. ἐρχομαι
30.	καταποντιζομαι	I sink
31.	ἐκτεινας	1 aor. part. 'having stretched out'
31.	ὀλιγοπιστος	of little faith
31.	εἰs τι	why?
31.	δισταζω	I doubt
32.	ἀναβαντων αὐτων	correct genitive absolute: 'when they had climbed...'
32.	κοπαζω	I cease, abate
33.	οἱ	they, the (men)

2. The Penitent Thief (Luke 23:39–43)

Basic Words

βλασφημεω	I abuse, insult (God or man)
οὐχι	not at all, not so (a more emphatic οὐ); used in a question expecting 'yes', as here.
σεαυτον (reflexive 2nd per. s.)	yourself
ἑτερος, -α, -ον	the other (second of pair) [*heterodox*]
ἐπιτιμαω	I rebuke (w. dat.); I warn, charge (w. ἱνα)
οὐδε (adv.) (conj.)	not even; and not, neither, nor
ἀξιος, -α -ον	worthy, deserving [*axiom*]
πρασσω (1 aor. ἐπραξα)	I act, do [*practical*]
μιμνησκομαι (1 aor. ἐμνησθην)	I remember (w. gen.) (here 1 aor. imp.)
ὁταν	whenever (w. subj. for indefinite future); when (w. indic.)
βασιλεια	sovereignty; kingdom, realm
ἀμην	indeed, certainly; Amen! So let it be!
σημερον	today

39.	κρεμασθεντων κρεμαννυμι	aor. pass. part. 'of the hanged' from
39.	κακουργος	evil-worker, criminal
40.	ἐφη	(inquit), 'quoth he', from φημι
40.	αὐτος	in this position means 'the same'
40.	κριμα, -ατος, το	condemnation
41.	μεν... δε	pointing the contrast
41.	δικαιως	justly
41.	ὠν	gen. pl. rel. pron. ὁς 'for what we did'
41.	ἀπολαμβανω	I get back
41.	ἀτοπος, -ον	out of place, improper
43.	ἐση	future of εἰμι sum
43.	παραδεισος	Paradise. A Persian word for park or garden, christianised for intermediate state of Church Expectant, as many believe.

3. The Call of Nathanael (John 1:43–51)

Basic Words

ἐπαυριον, αὐριον	on the morrow, tomorrow
ἀκολουθεω (w. dat.)	I follow, accompany [*acolyte*]
νομος	an ordinance; the Mosaic Law [*economy*]
ἀγαθος, -η -ον	good [*Agatha*]
ποθεν;	where from? (here: 'how?')
προ (prep. w. gen., time and place)	before; in front of [*prologue*]
φωνεω	I call, shout (here 1 aor. infin. w. article)
βασιλευς, -εως	a king [*Basil*]
μειζων, -ονος; μειζον (neut.)	greater (irreg. comp. μεγας)
οὐρανος	the sky; heaven [*Uranus*]
ἀνοιγω (1 aor. ἠνοιξα)	I open (here acc. sing. perf. part.)
ἀγγελος	a messenger, an angel

General Notes

43.	ἐξελθειν	2 aor. infin. ἐξερχομαι
45.	εὑρηκα	(perf.) εὑρισκω
46.	εἰναι	pres. infin. εἰμι
47.	δολος	deceit
48.	ὀντα	acc. m. sing. pres. part. εἰμι, agreeing w. σε
48.	συκη	a fig tree [*sycamore*]
50.	ὑποκατω	underneath
50.	τουτων	gen. of comparison: 'than these'
50.	ὀψομαι	future used for ὁραω

4. Picking Corn on the Sabbath (Mark 2:23–28)

Basic Words

σαββατον (and plur.)	the Sabbath
ὁδος, ἡ (Lat. *via*)	a road, way;
(Lat. *iter*)	a journey [*method*; *hodometer*]
ἐξεστιν (impers.)	it is permitted, lawful
οὐδεποτε	never
ἀναγινωσκω	I read
ὁτε	when, at which time (w. indic.)
χρεια	need, necessity
πειναω (1 aor. ἐπεινασα)	I hunger
πως;	how? (direct and indirect questions); how!
οἰκος	a house; household, family [*economy*]
ἀρχιερευς, -εως	high priest (also prob. used for 'chief priest')
ἀρτος	bread, a loaf; food
ἐσθιω (2 aor. ἐφαγον)	I eat
ἱερευς, -εως	a priest [*hierarchy*]

General Notes

23.	αὐτον... παραπορευεσθαι	
	lit. 'Him to go beside', articular infin., w. subject in acc.	
23.	τα σποριμα	the crops
23.	ἠρξαντο	from ἀρχομαι
23.	τιλλω	I pluck
23.	σταχυς	corn ear
24.	ὁ	neut. rel. pron.: that which, what
26.	ἐπι	(here) at the time of
26.	προθεσις	laying-out
26.	εἰ μη	but only, unless
26.	οὐσιν	dat. plur. pres. part. εἰμι
28.	ὡστε	consequently, and so

5. Introduction to Acts and the Promise of the Holy Spirit (Acts 1:1–5)

The student is strongly advised to follow this text with the RV or RSV, as the Greek is involved for the beginner.

Basic Words

πρωτος, -η, -ον	first (see GV) [*prototype*]
διδασκω (1 aor. ἐδιδαξα)	I teach [*didactic*]
ἀχρι (prep. w. gen.)	until (time and space)
ἐντελλομαι (1 aor. ἐνετειλαμην)	I instruct, command
ἀποστολος	a messenger, delegate, apostle
ἐκλεγομαι (1 aor. ἐξελεξαμην)	I choose, select [*eclectic*]
ἀγιος, -α, -ον	set-apart, holy, sacred [*hagiology*]
παριστημι	(*trans.* tenses: pres., fut., imperf., and 1 aor. παρεστησα) I place beside, present, provide (for *intrans.* aspect, see 'Ascension', no. 9)
ζαω	I live (here acc. sing., pres. Act. part.)
πασχω (2 aor. ἐπαθον)	I suffer [*pathology*] (see GV)
παραγγελλω (1 aor. παρηγγειλα)	I command
βαπτιζω	I dip, baptise

53

General Notes

2. ἀνελημφθη aor. pass. ἀναλαμβανω I take up (put after 'until which day')

2. ἐντειλαμενος having instructed

3. μετα w. acc. after

3. τεκμηριον proof, evidence

3. τεσσερακοντα forty

3. ὀπτανομαι I am seen

3. τα 'the things'

4. συναλιζομαι I meet with (or, I have meat with) sic!

4. χωριζομαι I depart

4. περιμενω I await

4. ἐπαγγελια a promise

4. ἡν ἡκουσατε direct speech

5. βαπτισθησεσθε fut. pass.

6. The Two Sons (Matthew 21:28–32)

Basic Words

δοκεω	I suppose, think; I seem, am thought.
δοκει (impers. w. dat.)	it seems [*Docetism*]
τεκνον	child (see GV)
προσερχομαι	I come to, approach
ὑπαγω (see ἀγω)	I go away, withdraw
ἐργαζομαι (intrans.) (trans.)	I am at work, I work; I produce by work, I perform
ἀπερχομαι	I go away from, leave
δευτερος, -α, -ον	second [*Deuteronomy*]
δευτερον (adv.)	secondly
ὡσαυτως	similarly, likewise
θελημα, -ατος, το	the will [*monothelite*]
προαγω	I precede, go before; I lead forward

General Notes

28. εἶχεν imperf., continuous state

28. ἀμπελων, -ωνος   vineyard

29. understand ὑπαγω between ἐγω and κυριε

30. ὑστερον   later

30. μεταμελομαι I change mind

31. ὁ ὑστερος   the latter

31. τελωνης   tax-collector

31. πορνη   prostitute

32. δικαιοσυνη   righteousness

32. του w. infin. πιστευσαι indicating consequence here: 'so as to'

7. The First Temptation (Matthew 4:1–4)

Basic Words

ἀναγω (see ἀγω)	I lead up
ἐρημος, -ον (adj. used as *fem*. noun)	desolate; the desert [*hermit*]
πειραζω	I test; I tempt; I try (w. infin.) [*empirical; pirate*]
διαβολος	the devil, a slanderer [*diabolical*]
νυξ, νυκτος, ἡ	night
λιθος	stone [*palaeolithic*]
μονος, -η, -ον	alone, only [*monotheism*]
ῥημα, -ατος, το	spoken word [*rhetoric*]
ἐκπορευομαι	I journey out; I come forth
στομα, -ατος, το	mouth [*St Chrysostom = golden-mouth; colostomy*]

General Notes

1.	πειρασθηναι	aor. infin. pass.
2.	νηστευω	I fast; aor. part. act.
2.	τεσσαρακοντα	forty
2.	ἡμερας... νυκτας	acc. for length of time
2.	ὑστερον	afterwards
3.	ὁ πειραζων	'the tempting one,' tempter
3.	ἱνα w. subj.	for indirect command

8. The Second and Third Temptations (Matthew 4:5–11)

Basic Words

παραλαμβανω	I take with me; I receive from
ἱερον	a temple
βαλλω (2 aor. ἐβαλον)	I throw; I place, put [*ballistics*]
αἱρω (fut. ἀρω, 1 aor. ἠρα)	I raise; I carry; I remove
μηποτε	lest ever, lest perhaps
πους, ποδος, ὁ	foot [*chiropodist*]
παλιν (adv.)	again, moreover [*palindrome*]
ὀρος, ὀρους, το	a mountain
ὑψηλος, -η, -ον	high
ὑψιστος, -η, -ον	highest
ὑψος, -ους, το	height
ὑψοω	I raise to a height
λιαν	very, exceedingly
δεικνυμι (1 aor. ἐδειξα)	I show, point out
κοσμος	world, universe [*cosmic; cosmetic*]
δοξα	glory, honour [*doxology*] (see GV)

πιπτω (2 aor. ἐπεσον) I fall

ἀφιημι (1 aor. ἀφηκα) I leave alone; I forgive (see GV)

διακονεω I serve, wait at table [*diaconate*]

General Notes

5. ἐστησεν *trans.* 1 aor. ἱστημι

5. πτερυγιον gable, pinnacle

6. κατω downwards

6   ἐντειλεται fut. of 'liquid' vb. ἐντελλομαι

6. προσκοπτω I strike against

6. μηποτε προσκοψῃς final clause in primary sequence

7. ἐκπειραζω I put to thorough test

9. δωσω fut. διδωμι

9. πεσων aor. part. πιπτω

9. ἐαν w. aor. subj. for fut. condition

10. Σατανα voc. of Σατανας, Satan, which normally has article

10. λατρευω I serve, worship [*idolatry*]

9. The Ascension (Acts 1:6–12)

Basic Words

Again the student is recommended to follow with the RV or RSV

συνερχομαι	I come together; I accompany
χρονος	time; a period [*chronology*]
καιρος	season, time (see GV re 'God's time')
ἐξουσια	power, authority; (quasi-personally) spiritual or earthly 'power'
ἐσχατος, -η, -ον	last [*eschatology*]
ἐπαιρω	I raise up, lift up
ὀφθαλμος	an eye [*ophthalmic*]
παριστημι (*intrans. tenses*: perf., plup., and 2 aor. παρεστην)	I stand by, beside (this plup. w. imperf. sense); I appear; I am present (for *trans.* aspect, see no. 5)
θεαομαι (1 aor. ἐθεασαμην)	I look at, contemplate [*theatre*]
ὑποστρεφω	I turn back, return (intrans.)
καλεω (1 aor. ἐκαλεσα)	I call, summon, invite; I call, name
ἐγγυς (adv. and prep., mostly w. gen.)	near (time and place)

General Notes

6. ἠρωτων   imperf. contr. ἐρωταω

6. εἰ   (here) if, whether

6. ἀποκαθιστανω I restore, set up again

7. γνωναι   aor. infin. γινωσκω

7. ἐθετο   2 aor. mid. τιθημι

8. λημψεσθε   fut. λαμβανω

8. ἐπελθοντος Ἁγιου Πνευματος genitive absolute

8. μαρτυς, -υρος witness; martyr

9. βλεποντων αὑτων   genitive absolute

9. νεφελη   a cloud

9. ὑπολαμβανω I take up

10. πορευομενου αὑτου   genitive absolute

10. ἀτενιζω   I gaze

10. ἐσθης, -ητος, ἡ clothing

10. λευκος   white [*leukaemia*]

11. ἀναλημφθεις aor. part. pass. ἀναλαμβανω

11. τροπος   manner, way

12. ἐχον   n. part. = ὁρος

10. The High Priestly Prayer (John 17:1–7)

Basic Words

ὥρα	an hour; time [*horology*]
δοξαζω	I praise, magnify; I glorify [*doxology*]
καθως	even as…, just as…
ζωη	life (physical or spiritual) [*Zoë*; cf. *Zoology*]
αἰωνιος, -ον	age-long, eternal
ἀληθινος, -η, -ον	true, real, genuine
ἐργον	work, labour; (more often) action, deed [*energy*]
τηρεω	I guard, preserve; (of regulations) I observe, obey
ὁσος, -η, -ον	how much/many; how great (see GV)

General Notes

1.	ἐληλυθεν	perf. ἐρχομαι
2.	σαρξ, σαρκος, ἡ	flesh
2.	δωσῃ	1 aor. subj. διδωμι
3.	ἱνα γινωσκωσιν	consider as an infin., rather than a final clause
4.	τελειοω	I complete, perfect
5.	παρα	w. dat. beside, with
5.	εἰχον	imperf. for continuous state
5.	εἰναι	pres. infin. εἰμι 'was'
6.	φανεροω	I make clear, visible
6.	κἀμοι	and... to me
7.	παρα	w. gen. from (w. persons)

11. The Widow's Son at Nain
(Luke 7:11–17)

Basic Words

ὀχλος	crowd; common people, mob (*ochlocracy*: mob-rule)
ἐγγιζω	I come near, approach
ἀποθνησκω (2 aor. ἀπεθανον)	I die (here as perf. part., 'a – having – died – man')
μητηρ, -ρος, ἡ	mother [*metropolis*]
χηρα	a widow
ἱκανος, -η, -ον	considerable, sufficient; worthy, suitable
σπλαγχνιζομαι	I feel sorry for
σπλαγχνα (n. pl.)	compassion, pity
κλαιω (1 aor. ἐκλαυσα)	I weep, lament (for)
ἁπτομαι (1 aor. ἡψαμην)	(w. gen.) I touch, take hold of
βασταζω	I carry (off); bear, endure
ἐγειρω (1 aor. ἠγειρα)	I wake, I arouse; I raise up (here aor. pass. imp.)
νεκρος, -α, -ον (adj.) (noun)	dead; the dead, a corpse [*necropolis*]
φοβος	fear (sometimes reverential), terror [*phobia*]

μεγας, μεγαλη, μεγα	large, great [*megaphone*]
ὁλος, -η, -ον	whole, all [*holocaust*]

General Notes

11.	ἑξης (adv.)	next (day)
12.	πυλη	gate [*pylon*]
12.	ἐκκομιζω	I carry out
12.	μονογενης	only-born
14.	σορος (fem.)	funeral bier
14.	νεανισκος	youth (here voc.)
15.	ἀνακαθιζω	I sit up
16.	ἐπισκεπτομαι	I visit
17.	περιχωρος, ἡ	(γη understood) neighbourhood, district

12. Taking up the Cross (Mark 8:34–9:1)

Basic Words

προσκαλεομαι	I call to myself
ὀπισω (adv. and prep. w. gen.)	behind; after (see GV)
ἀρνεομαι and ἀπαρνεομαι	I deny; I disown
σταυρος	a cross, the crucifixion
σταυροω	I crucify
ψυχη	life; soul; self [*psychology*]
ἀπολλυμι (1 aor. ἀπωλεσα) (here fut.) (mid.)	I destroy completely; I lose utterly; I perish, am lost [*Apollyon; Apollo?*]
ἐνεκεν (prep. w. gen.)	on account of, for sake of
ἐμος, -η, -ον	my, mine
γενεα	a generation (genealogy)
μοιχευω	I commit adultery
μοιχεια	adultery
μοιχος	adulterer
μοιχαλις, -ιδος	adulteress; disloyal (adj.)
ἁμαρτωλος, -ον (adj.) (noun)	sinful; a sinner
ὡδε (adv.)	here (rest); hither (motion)

ὅστις	(ὅς and τις both declined as with 'Respublica', but it is chiefly nom.) who, which (generic) – 'as other like persons, things'; who, which (essential) – 'by his, her, its very nature';
w. ἄν (ἐάν) and subj.	whosoever (see GV)
γευομαι (1 aor. ἐγευσαμην)	I taste; (fig.) I experience
θανατος	death [*euthanasia*]

General Notes

34.	ἀπαρνησασθω	1 aor. mid. imp.
34.	ἀρατω	1 aor. act. imp. αἱρω
34.	ἀκολουθειτω	pres. imp. for continuous action
35.	ὅς... ἐαν	and subj.: indef. 'whoever'
35.	εὐαγγελιον	good news, gospel
36.	ὠφελεω	I benefit, help
36.	κερδαινω	I gain (aor. act. infin.)
36.	ζημιοω	(in pass.) I forfeit, lose (aor. pass. infin.)
37.	δοι	optative, from διδωμι 'what could/is he to give?'
37.	ἀνταλλαγμα	an exchange
38.	ἐπαισχυνομαι	I am ashamed of
9:1.	ἐστηκοτων	gen. plur. perf. part. act. ἱστημι

68

9:1. Again, οὐ μη and aor. subj. introduces strong negative future assertion.

9:1. ἐως ἀν   (until) and aor. subj. for indef. fut.

9:1. ἐληλυθυιαν   fem. acc. sing. perf. part. act. ἐρχομαι

13. The Baptist's Question (Luke 7:18–23)

Basic Words

ἀπαγγελλω(1 aor. ἀπηγγειλα)   I report, announce

πεμπω (1 aor. ἐπεμψα)   I send [*pomp*]

ἀλλος, -η, -ο   other, another (see GV) [*allegory*]

προσδοκαω (and προσδεχομαι) I expect, await (see GV)

παραγινομαι (2 aor. -εγενομην) I come near, arrive at

θεραπευω   (I serve, I treat) I heal, cure [*therapy*]

πονηρος, -α, -ον   wicked; the Evil one, evil (See GV)

τυφλος, -η, -ον   blind

ἀναβλεπω   I recover sight; I look up

χωλος, -η, -ον   lame

καθαριζω   I cleanse, make clean

πτωχος,-η,-ον   poor; a beggar

εὐαγγελιζω   I proclaim good news; I preach the Gospel

μακαριος, -α, -ον   happy, blessed [*Archbishop Makarios*]

σκανδαλιζω   I repel, offend [*scandal*]

General Notes

19.	ὁ ἐρχομενος	'the coming one'
19.	προδοκωμεν	deliberative subj.: 'are we to expect?'
20.	εἰπαν	1 aor. ending on 2 aor. form
21.	ἡ νοσος	disease
21.	ἡ μαστιξ	(alleged) God-sent illness (heavy whip)
21.	χαριζομαι	I graciously give
22.	λεπρος	a leper
22.	κωφος	blunt, dull; deaf; dumb
23.	ὁς ἐαν	and subj. indef. 'whoever'

14. The Nobleman's Son (John 4:46–end)

Basic Words

ὁπου	where; to where (see GV)
οἰνος	wine
ἀσθενεω	(not strong) I am weak; I am sick [*neurasthenia*]
ἡκω (fut. ἡξω)	I have come, am present
ἰαομαι (1 aor. ἰασαμην)	I heal, cure [*psychiatrist*]
μελλω	I am about to…, I intend… (w. infin.) (see GV)
σημειον	a sign; a miracle [*semantic*; *semaphore*]
τερας, -ατος, το	a wonder, marvel
παιδιον	little boy, child (see GV)
ἡδη	now, already
δουλος	slave, bondservant
οἰκια	a house, household [*economy*]

General Notes

46.	βασιλικος	royal official
46.	οὐ	whose – gen. rel. pron.
47.	ἱνα	introducing noun clause for indir. command
48.	οὐ μη	and aor. subj. again, for strong future neg. assertion
49.	καταβηθι	irreg. imp. καταβαινω
49.	πριν and infin.	before
51.	αὐτου καταβαινοντος	non-classical gen. abs.
51.	ὑπανταω	I meet
52.	πυνθανομαι	I enquire
52.	κομψοτερον ἐσχεν	'he got better'
52.	ἐχθες	yesterday
52.	ἐβδομος	seventh
52.	πυρετος	fever

15. The Spine-Curvature Miracle
(Luke 13:10–17)

Basic Words

μια (fem. of εἱς)	one
συναγωγη	assembly, synagogue
ἐτος, -ους, το (and ἐνιαυτος, ὁ)	a year [*Etesian wind*]
ἀπολυω	I let loose, release; I dismiss, divorce
ἐπιτιθημι	I place, lay upon
ἐξ	six [*hexagon*]
δει (impers.)	it is necessary, one must (imperf. ἐδει)
ἐκαστος, -η, -ον	each, every (of more than two)
λυω	I unloose, release; (fig.) I break up, destroy [*analysis*]
ποτιζω	I cause to drink
ποτηριον	a cup (cf. potion)
θυγατηρ, -τρος	daughter
δεω	I bind, tie (dist. from δεομαι) [*arthrodesis*]
δεσμος, δεσμα(n. pl.)	a bond, chain
χαιρω (2 aor. ἐχαρην, in act. sense)	I rejoice, am glad; (imp. for greetings: 'Hail!')

General Notes

11.	ἀσθενεια	(not-strength) weakness
11.	συνκυπτω	I am bent double
11.	ἀνακυπτω	I raise myself
11.	εἰς το παντελες completely, utterly	
13.	παραχρημα	(Lucan) immediately
13.	ἀνορθοω	I make straight again [*orthopaedic*]
14.	ἀγανακτεω	I am indignant
15.	βους	ox
15.	ὀνος	ass
15.	φατνη	manger, trough
15.	ἀπαγω	I lead away
16.	start w. οὐκ ἐδει, then ταυτην: 'ought not this (woman), being a daughter…'	
17.	καταισχυνω	I shame
17.	ἀντικειμαι	I resist, oppose
17.	ἐνδοξος, -ον	glorious
17.	τα γινομενα	'the things happening/coming about'

16. The Ten Bridesmaids
(Matthew 25:1–13)

Basic Words

ὁμοιοω	I make like, compare (fut. pass. here)
ὁμοιος, -α, -ον	like, similar [*homoeopathy*]
πεντε, οἱ, αἱ, τα	five [*pentagon*]
ἐλαιον	olive oil
ἐλαια	olive tree
μεσος, -η, -ον	middle, in the middle [*Mesopotamia*]
μαλλον	(the) more, rather
πωλεω (and πιπρασκω)	I sell [*monopoly*]
ἀγοραζω	I buy
ἐτοιμος, -η, -ον	ready, prepared
θυρα	door [indir., *thyroid*]
λοιπος, -η, -ον	the remaining, the rest (see GV)
γρηγορεω	I am on the watch, alert [*Gregory*]

General Notes

1. αἵτινες   fem. plur. ὅστις who
1. λαβουσαι   fem. aor. part.
1. λαμπας   lantern
1. ὑπαντησις   reception, meeting
1. νυμφιος   bridegroom
2. μωρος   foolish [*moron*]
2. φρονιμος, -ον sensible, prudent
4. ἀγγειον   flask, container
5. χρονιζοντος νυμφιου   'while the bridegroom delayed' (gen. abs.)
5. νυσταζω   I am drowsy;
    καθευδω   I sleep
6. κραυγη   shout
7. κοσμεω   I adjust, trim [*cosmetic*]
8. δοτε   aor. imp. διδωμι
8. σβεννυμι   I extinguish
9. ἀρκεω   I am sufficient
10. γαμοι   (plur.) wedding-feast
10. κλειω   I shut
11. ὑστερον   later

17. John the Baptist's Ministry (Mark 1:1–5)

Basic Words

ἀρχη	beginning; rule [*archaeology; monarchy*]
προσωπον	human face, look; presence (see GV)
ἑτοιμαζω	I prepare, make ready
κηρυσσω	I proclaim, herald, preach
βαπτισμα, -ατος, το	immersion, baptism
μετανοια	change of mind, repentance
ἀφεσις, -εως, ἡ	remission, forgiveness
ἁμαρτια	sin
χωρα	land, region, (the) country
χωριον	piece of land, property
ὁμολογεω	I confess, admit, declare (See GV; and Lexicon for nuances and similar ἐξομολογεω)

General Notes

1. εὐαγγελιον   good news, Gospel
2. κατασκευαζω I prepare, build
3. βοαω   I shout, call out
3. εὐθυς, -εια, -υ   straight
3. τριβος, ἡ   path
4. εἰς   (here) for
5. ποταμος   river [*hippopotamus*]

18. The Reaction to Peter's Sermon (Acts 2:36–42a)

Basic Words

καρδια	heart; mind; will (see GV) [*cardiac*]
μετανοεω	I change mind, repent
δωρον and δωρεα δωρεαν (adv. acc.)	a gift [*Dora, Theodore*]
μακραν (adv.)	at a distance
μακροθεν (adv.)	from a distance
πλειων, πλειον (n.) (adj.) (noun)	(comp. of πολυς) more; larger the greater number, the more
προστιθημι	I place/put to, I add, join to [*prosthesis*]
ὡσει	as if, as it were; (w. numbers) about
διδαχη	teaching, doctrine [*didactic*]

General Notes

36. ἀσφαλως   assuredly
36. γινωσκετω   imp. 'let... know'
37. κατανυσσομαι   I am 'pierced'
37. ποιησωμεν   delib. subj. 'what are we to do?'
38. λημψεσθε   fut. λαμβανω
39. ἐπαγγελια   promise
40. διαμαρτυρομαι   I testify solemnly
40. παρακαλεω   I exhort, implore
40. σωθητε   aor. imp. pass. σῳζω
40. σκολιος   crooked, perverse
41. ἀποδεχομαι   I receive, welcome
41. τρισχιλιοι, -αι, -α   three thousand
42. προσκαρτερεω   I continue, persevere

19. St. John's Prologue (John 1:4–13)

Basic Words

σκοτος, -ους, το and σκοτια, ἡ	darkness [*scotoscope*]
φαινω (act.) (pass.)	I give light, shine; I appear, become visible
καταλαμβανω (mid.)	I lay hold of, seize; I overtake; I comprehend
μαρτυριον, το and μαρτυρια, ἡ	witness, evidence, testimony [*martyr*]
μαρτυρεω	I witness, give evidence, testify
αἱμα, -ατος, το	blood [*haemorrhage*]
γενναω (pass.)	I beget, bring forth; [*hydrogen*] I am born

General Notes

4. γεγονεν   perf. γινομαι

6. ἀπεσταλμενος   perf. pass. part. ἀποστελλω

7. ἱνα and subjunctives 'in order that' (final)

9. φωτιζω   I enlighten

9. either ἐρχομενον is nom. neut. agreeing w. φως, or (less likely?) it is acc. masc. agreeing with w. ἀνθρωπον – the older interpretation.

10. και (here)   even (?)

10. ἐγνω   2 aor. γινωσκω

12. πιστευουσιν   dat. pl. agreeing w. αὐτοις

13. σαρξ, σαρκος, ἡ   flesh (*sarcasm; sarcophagus*)

20. The Hidden Treasure and the Pearl Merchant (Matthew 13:44–46)

Basic Words

θησαυριζω	I treasure up
θησαυρος	a store, treasure [*thesaurus*]
ἀγρος	a field; the country; [cf. *agriculture*] (plur.) lands, farms (see GV)
κρυπτος, -η, -ον	hidden, secret [*crypt*]
κρυπτω	I hide, conceal
χαρα	joy, delight
ζητεω and ἐπιζητεω	I search for, seek
καλος, -η, -ον	good (and seen to be so, cf. ἀγαθος) [*calligraphy*]

General Notes

44.	κεκρυμμενῳ	dat. perf. pass. part. κρυπτω
44.	εὑρων	aor. part. εὑριοκω
45.	ἐμπορος	trader, merchant [*emporium*]
45.	ζητουντι	dat. pres. part.
45.	μαργαριτης	pearl [*Margaret*]
46.	πολυτιμος	costly, expensive
46.	πεπρακεν	perf. act. πιπρασκω
46.	εἰχεν	imp. for continuous action

21. The Drag-Net; The Christian Scribe (Matthew 13:47–52)

Basic Words

θαλσσα, -ης	sea
συναγω	I gather together, collect [*synagogue*]
πληροω	I fulfil, complete, accomplish
καθιζω (intrans.)	I sit (down), am seated; [cf. *cathedral*]
(rarely trans.)	I seat; I appoint
ἐξω (adv.)	out, outside (sometimes w. art.)
(prep. w. gen.)	out of
αἰων, -ωνος, ὁ	era, age, time-cycle (see GV) [*aeon*]
δικαιος, -α, -ον	righteous, just
πυρ, πυρος, το	fire (see GV) [*pyrotechnics*]
ἐκει (adv.)	there; thither, there (w. verbs of motion)
συνιημι (1 aor. συνηκα)	I understand, perceive
ναι	yes
ἐκβαλλω	I throw out, expel, exorcise; (in weaker sense) I take out, remove
καινος, -η, -ον	new, fresh, novel (see GV)

General Notes

47.	βληθεισῃ	aor. pass. part. βαλλω
47.	γενος, -ους	sort, kind
47.	συναγαγουσῃ	2 aor. part., also agreeing w. drag-net
48.	ἀναβιβαζω	I bring up
48.	αἰγιαλος	beach, shore
48.	συλλεγω	I collect, gather together
48.	ἀγγος	container, vessel
48.	σαπρος	worthless, decayed
49.	συντελεια	consummation, end
49.	ἐξελευσονται	fut. of ἐξερχομαι
49.	ἀφοριζω	I separate
50.	βαλουσιν	fut. βαλλω
50.	καμινος, ἡ	furnace
50.	κλαυθμος και βρυγμος	weeping and crunching
50.	ὁδους, -οντος	tooth [*orthodontist*]
52.	μαθητευθεις	having-been-made-a-disciple
52.	παλαιος	old [*palaeolithic*]

22. On Returning Good for Evil
(Luke 6:27–31)

Basic Words

ἀγαπαω	I love (see GV)
ἐχθρος, -α, -ον	(adj. hating, hostile – used often as noun) an enemy.
καλως	well, rightly, honourably
μισεω	I hate [*misogynist*]
εὐλογεω	(lit. 'I speak well') I bless; I praise [*eulogy*]
προσευχομαι	I pray (w. acc. 'for', but see GV)
τυπτω	I strike, beat [*type*]
παρεχω	(act. and mid.) I show, cause (w. immaterial things); I present, supply
ἱματιον	outer garment, cloak; (plur.) clothing
κωλυω	I prevent, hinder (w. inf.: 'from…')
αἰτεω	I ask, request;
(mid.)	I ask for myself
σος, ση, σον	your (2nd pers. sing.), thy, thine
ὁμοιως	similarly, likewise

General Notes

27.	τοις ἀκουουσιν	dat. plur. pres. part. agreeing w. ὑμιν
28.	καταραομαι	I curse
28.	ἐπηρεαζω	I mistreat, abuse
29.	τυπτοντι	dat. pres. part., 'to him striking you.'
29.	σιαγων, -ονος, ἡ	cheek, jaw
29.	χιτων, -ωνος, ὁ	tunic, undergarment
29.	μη κωλυσῃς	aor. subj. for prohibition
30.	διδου	pres. imp. 'always give'
30.	αἰτουντι	dat. pres. part., lit. 'to every him asking'
30.	ἀπαιτεω	I ask back
30.	σα (n. pl.)	your things

23. The Rich Fool (Luke 12:13–19)

Basic Words

διδασκαλος	a teacher [*didactic*]
κριτης	a judge [*critic*]
φυλασσω	I guard, watch, protect; [*prophylactic*] I keep, observe
ὑπαρχω	I am; I belong to
τα ὑπαρχοντα	one's possessions (see GV)
παραβολη	an allegory, parable
πλουσιος, -α, -ον	rich, wealthy
διαλογιζομαι	I consider, argue
διαλογισμος	reasoning, plotting
που;	where? where to? (whither?)
καρπος	fruit; deed, result; profit [*Polycarp*]
οἰκοδομεω	I build (a house); (hence fig.)
κειμαι	I have been placed; I lie (perf. used as pass. of τιθημι)
πινω (2 aor. ἐπιον)	I drink

General Notes

13.	μεριζω	I divide, share
13.	κληρονομια	inheritance
14.	καθιστημι	I appoint
14.	μεριστης	a divider
15.	πλεονεξια	covetousness
15.	περισσευω	I exceed, overflow
16.	εὐφορεω	I bear well
18.	καθελω	fut. of καθαιρεω I pull down
18.	ἀποθηκη	store-house, barn
18.	σιτος	corn
19.	ἐρω	fut. of λεγω
19.	ἀναπαυομαι	I rest
19.	φαγε	aor. imp. of ἐσθιω
19.	εὐφραινομαι	I make merry

24. Miracles at Capernaum (Mark 1:27–35)

Basic Words

ἁπας	quite all, the whole (see πας)
ὡστε	1. so that, so as to (w. infin. in consecutive clauses; neg. μη)
	2. so then, consequently (w. a main clause in indic. or imper., w. result stated merely as a new fact; neg. οὐ)
ἀκαθαρτος, -ον	unclean, impure
ἀκοη	hearing, ear; report, rumour
κρατεω	(I am powerful) I take hold of, obtain [*democrat*]
ὀψια	twilight, dusk
ἡλιος	the sun [*heliograph*; *heliotrope*]
κακος, -η, -ον	bad, evil [*cacophony*]
κακως	badly, evilly, ill
δαιμονιον	evil spirit, demon
πρωϊ (adv.)	early
πρωια, ἡ	early morning
ἀνιστημι	I raise up, set up (*trans*. fut. and 1 aor.); I rise (*intr*. middle and 2 aor.)
τοπος	place [*topic; topography*]

General Notes

27.	θαμβεω	I amaze
27.	συνζητεω	I discuss, argue
27.	ἐπιτασσω	I order, command
27.	ὑπακουω	I obey
28.	πανταχου	everywhere
28.	περιχωρος, ἡ	neighbourhood
30.	πενθερα	mother-in-law
30.	κατακειμαι	I am lying (ill)
30.	πυρεσσω	I have fever
31.	πυρετος	a fever
32.	δυνω	I sink (intr.)
32.	κακως ἐχοντας	'having badly', be ill
32.	δαιμονιζομαι	I am demon-possessed
33.	ἐπισυναγω	I collect, gather
34.	ποικιλος	various
34.	νοσος, ἡ	disease
34.	ἠδεισαν	pluperfect of οἰδα, prob. w. imperfect meaning
35.	ἐννυχα	in the night

25. Peter, John, and the Sanhedrin (Acts 4:13–20)

Basic Words

θεωρεω	I look at, gaze; I see, perceive [*theory; theorem*]
παρρησια	free speech; confidence, boldness
θαυμαζω (intr.) (trans.)	I am astonished, surprised; I admire, wonder at
ἐπιγινωσκω	I know accurately; I recognise, perceive; I discover
συνεδριον	Council of seventy-one members at Jerusalem; a local Jewish tribunal
ἀλληλους, -ων, -οις	one another (see GV)
γνωστος, -η, -ον	known; an acquaintance
κατοικεω (trans.) (intr.)	I inhabit, live in; I settle, dwell
μηκετι	no longer
μηδεις, -εμια, -εν (adj.) (noun) (neut.)	no, none; (m. and f.) no person, nobody; nothing
μηδε (conj.) (adv.)	but not, and not, neither/nor; not even

ἐνωπιον (prep. w. gen.)   in presence of, before

κρινω   I decide, determine;
I judge (privately or in law-court);
I condemn

General Notes

13. ἀγαμματος   illiterate

13. ἰδιωτης   amateur, layman

14. τον ἀνθρωπον cured lame beggar

14. ἐστωτα   acc. perf. part. ἰστημι

14. τεθεραπευμενον perf. pass. part. 'healed'

14. ἐχω and infin.   I am able to...

14. ἀντειπειν   aor. infin. ἀντιλεγω

15. κελευω   I command, order

15. συνβαλλω (λογους) I discuss

16. φανερος   clear, evident

17. ἱνα μη   lest (final clause)

17. ἐπι πλειον   more

17. διανεμω   I spread about

17. ἀπειλεω   I threaten
(exhortation in subjunctive)

18. καθολου   at all

18. φθεγγομαι   I utter

20. 'For we are unable not to speak...'

26. The Cleansing of the Temple (John 2:13–22)

Basic Words

πασχα (only article το declines)   Passover feast

προβατον   a sheep

καθημαι   I am seated, I sit

ἐκχεω, ἐκχυνω   I pour out, shed, spill

τραπεζα   a table [*trapezium, trapeze*]

ἐντευθεν (adv.)   from here, hence

ναος   a temple; an inner shrine (see ἱερον)

τρεις, τρια (n.)   three [*triad*]

γραφη   a writing; Scripture text; Old Testament Scriptures (pl.)

General Notes

14.	βους	an ox
14.	περιστερα	a dove
14.	κερματιστης	a money-changer
15.	φραγελλιον	a small lash
15.	σχοινιον	rope, cord
15.	κολλυβιστης	a money-changer
15.	κερμα	a small coin
15.	ἀναστρεφω	I overturn
16.	τοις πωλουσιν	dat. part. 'to those who sold'
16.	ἐμποριον	market
17.	γεγραμμενον ἐστιν	periphrastic perf. γραφω
17.	ζηλος	enthusiasm, fervour [zeal]
17.	καταφαγεται	from κατεσθιω I eat up, devour
19.	ἐγερω	fut. of 'liquid vb.' ἐγειρω
20.	τεσσερακοντα και ἑξ	forty-six

27. The Sheep and the Goats
(Matthew 25:31–36)

Basic Words

ἐμπροσθεν (adv., but mostly prep. w. gen.)	before, in front (of), in presence of
ἐθνος, -ους, το	people, race;
τα ἐθνη	nations, Gentiles [*ethnology*; *ethnic*]
ὡσπερ	just as, even as (περ, an enclitic particle, adds intensive force or positiveness to the word to which it is joined – indeed, by far, altogether.)
ποιμαινω	I shepherd, tend
ποιμην, -ενος	shepherd
ποιμνη (also -ιον)	flock
δεξιος, -α, -ον	(on) the right hand, right [via Latin, *dexterous*]
δευρο, δευτε	(sing. and plur. respect.; adverbs used as imperatives) Here! Come!
φυλακη	a prison; (a) guard; a watch of night [*prophylactic*]

General Notes

31.	θρονος	throne, seat
32.	συναχθησονται	fut. pass. συναγω
32.	ἀφοριζω	I separate (fut.)
32.	ἐριφος, το	goat
33.	στησει	trans. fut. ἱστημι
33.	εὐωνυμος	(well-named) left
34.	ἐρει	irreg. fut. of λεγω
34.	εὐλογημενοι	pres. part. pass
34.	κληρονομεω	I inherit
34.	ἡτοιμασμενην	perf. part. pass. ἐτοιμαζω
34.	καταβολη	foundation
35.	φαγειν	aor. infin. ἐσθιω
35.	διψαω	I thirst [*dipsomania*]
35.	ξενος	foreigner, stranger
35.	ἡμην	alternative imperf. εἰμι
36.	γυμνος	(half-) naked [*gymnasium*]
36.	περιβαλλω	(I throw around) I clothe
36.	ἐπισκεπτομαι	I visit

28. The Clever Steward (Luke 16:1–8a)

Basic Words

ἀποδιδωμι	I give back, restore; I render as due
ἐτι (adv.)	(time) still, (as) yet, even now; (degree) more, further, even, still
ἰσχυω	I have strength, prevail; I am able, I can (w. infin.)
δεχομαι	I receive, accept; I welcome
ποσος, -η, -ον;	how much/many? how great?
γραμμα, -ατος, το	letter of alphabet, writings, document

General Notes

1. οἰκονομος — steward
1. διαβαλλω — I slander, complain of
1. διασκορπιζω — I scatter, squander
3. ἀφαιρεω — I take away
3. σκαπτω — I dig
3. ἐπαιτεω — I beg
4. ἐγνων — aor. γινωσκω in a present sense
4. μετασταθω — from μεθιστημι I transfer, remove
5. χρεοφειλετης — a debtor
5. ὀφειλω — I owe; I ought
6. βατος — measure of eight to nine gallons
6. δεξαι — imp. of δεχομαι
6. ταχεως — quickly
7. κορος — ten to twelve bushels
7. σιτος — corn
8. ἐπαινεω — I praise, commend
8. ἀδικια — dishonesty
8. φρονιμως — shrewdly

29. The Centurion's Faith (Luke 7:1–10)[*]

Basic Words

πρεσβυτερος	an Elder; the elder (of two) [*presbyter*] (see GV)
ὁπως	in order that (w. subj. ± ἀν) (see GV)
φιλος	a friend [*bibliophile*]
ἐμαυτον, -ου, -ῳ	(reflexive and so no nom.) myself
παις, παιδος	child; male slave, servant [*pedagogue; orthopaedic*]
στρατευμα, -ατος, το	an army
στρατευομαι	I serve in army, make war
στρατιωτης	soldier
στρεφω	I turn; I turn myself (pass. reflex.)
τοσουτος, -αυτη, -ουτο(ν)	so great; so much, so many
πιστις, -εως, ἡ	faith, belief, trust; the (Christian) Faith
ὑγιαινω	I am well, sound
ὑγιης, -ες	healthy, sound [*hygiene*]

---

[*]This narrative from the alleged 'Q' is in both Luke and Matthew but the Lucan version has a wider vocabulary, even if a harder text.

General Notes

2.	ἑκατοναρχης	= κεντουριων
2.	τελευταω	I end, die
2.	ἐντιμος	precious, honoured
3.	διασῳζω	I save 'through', I completely heal?
4.	παρακαλεω	I ask, beg
4.	σπουδαιως	earnestly
4.	ᾡ παρεξῃ τουτο	'for whom he should do this'
6.	ἀπεχω	I am distant from
6.	σκυλλω	I worry, trouble
6.	στεγη	roof
7.	διο	therefore
7.	ἀξιοω	I treat as worthy
7.	ἰαθητω	aor. imp. pass. from ἰαομαι: 'let him be healed.'
8.	τασσω	I assign, appoint (pres. part. pass. n.)
9.	ἀκολουθουντι	dat. pres. part. act. w. ὀχλῳ
10.	πεμφθεντες	aor. pass. part. 'those who had been sent'
10.	ὑγιαινοντα	acc. pres. part. w. δουλον

30. The Rejection at Nazareth (Mark 6:1–7)

Basic Words

ἐκειθεν	(adv.) from there
σοφια	wisdom (divine and human) [*philosophy;* cf. *sophomore*]
τοιουτος, -αυτη, -ουτο(ν)	of such a kind, such
ἀδελφη	a sister; a Christian woman
ὀλιγος, -η, -ον	(pl.) few; (s.) small, short. slight [*oligarchy*]
κωμη	a village, small town
δωδεκα	(the) twelve (apostles) [*dodecagon*]

General Notes

1. πατρις, -ιδος, ἡ native place
2. ἐκπλησσομαι I am astounded
2. δοθεισα f. aor. part. pass. διδωμι
3. τεκτων a carpenter, artificer
4. ἀτιμος unhonoured
4. συγγενευς relation
5. ἀρρωστος infirm, ill
6. ἀπιστια unbelief
6. περιαγω I go about
6. κυκλος a circle [*cycle*]

31. The Death of Stephen (Acts 7:51–8:3)

(Use RV or RSV as crib, for vocabulary is large and rare)

Basic Words

οὖς, ὠτος, το	ear [*otology*]
ἀποκτεινω (1 aor. ἀπεκτεινα)	I kill
φονευς	a murderer
φονευω	I murder
φονος	murder
πληρης, -ες	full (sometimes not declined)
λιθαζω, λιθοβολεω	I stone
ἐπικαλεω (mid.)	I surname, nickname; I call upon, appeal to
κοιμαομαι	I fall asleep, I am asleep [*cemetery*]
ἐκκλησια	assembly; church [*ecclesiastic*] (see GV)
πλην (conj.) (prep. w. gen.)	however, nevertheless; except, apart from
παραδιδωμι (1 aor. παρεδωκα)	I hand over; I deliver up, betray; I hand down

General Notes

52.	διωκω	I pursue; I persecute
52.	προκαταγγελλω	I announce beforehand
53.	διαταγη	ordinance
55.	ἀτενιζω	I gaze
55.	ἑστωτα	acc. perf. part. ἱστημι
56.	διηνοιγμενους	acc. perf. part. pass. διανοιγω
57.	ὁρμαω	I rush, stampede [*hormone*]
57.	ὁμοθυμαδον	with one mind, accord
59.	ἐπικαλουμενον and λεγοντα acc. pres. parts. = Στεφανον	
60.	θεις (from τιθημι) γονατα *lit.*	'having placed his knees'
60.	μη στησῃς	aor. subj. ἱστημι for neg. imperative
1.	διασπειρω	I scatter
1.	κατα (distributive)	throughout
3.	συρω	I drag, pull

32. The Woman of Samaria (John 4:1–42)

Note: as the basic vocabulary diminishes, it naturally becomes increasingly hard to locate short passages containing the new words required. It is hoped, therefore, that the student will feel ready by now to cope with longer texts. The general notes will deal more with accidence and syntax than with vocabulary.

Basic Words

γε	indeed, really (emphatic particle)
διερχομαι	I go through, pass through
τροφη	nourishment, food [*atrophy*]
τρεφω	I feed, nourish
ἀληθης, -ες	true (things), truthful (persons)
οὐτε	and not, neither, nor;
οὐτε... οὐτε	neither... nor
ἀληθεια	truth (in widest sense)
ἀναγγελλω	I report; I announce
μητι	interrog. part. expecting negative answer and used in hesitant questions
θεριζω	I reap
θερισμος	harvest
μισθος	pay, wages; reward, recompense
σπειρω	I sow

σπερμα, -ατος, το	seed; offspring [*sperm*]
μενω (1 aor. ἐμεινα)	I remain, stay [cf. *permanent*]
	(numerous compounds)
οὐκετι	no longer, no more

General Notes

6.	κεκοπιακως	perf. part. κοπιαω
7.	δος	aor. imper. διδωμι
7.	πειν	late aor. infin. πινω
8.	ἀπεληλυθεισαν	plup. ἀπερχομαι
9.	ὠν... οὐσης	pres. parts. εἰμι
10.	ἠδεις	imperf. οἰδα
10.	ἀν	for unfulfilled condition
12.	μη	expecting 'No'
12.	του πατρος	genitive of comparison
14.	δωσω	fut. διδωμι
14.	οὐ μη	and aor. subj. or fut. indic. for strong negative future
23.	'He seeks such worshipping Him'	
32.	φαγε	aor. imp. ἐσθιω
33.	ἠνεγκεν	2 aor. indic. φερω
38.	κεκοπιακατε and κεκοπιακασιν	
		perf. indic. κοπιαω (in diff. sense from v.6)
38.	εἰσεληλυθατε	perf. indic. εἰσερχομαι
41.	πλειους	contracted from πλειονες

33. The Walk to Emmaus (Luke 24:13–43)

Basic Words

ποιος, -α, -ον;	what sort of? what?
δυνατος, -η, -ον	powerful, strong; able to (w. infin.); possible (n. δυνατον)
ἀρχων, -οντος	ruler, governor (see GV)
τριτος, -η, -ον	third (τριτον thirdly) [*Trito – Isaiah*]
ἐξιστημι (trans.) (intrans.)	I astonish; I am astonished; I am mad
μνημειον	a monument, a tomb
οὑ	where; (sometimes) where to, whither
ταρασσω	I trouble, perplex
μερος, -ους, το	a share, portion; a part (see GV for phrases) [*polymer*]

General Notes

14.	perf. part.	συμβαινω
16.	του and infin.	w. consecutive force
17.	ἐσταθησαν	aor. pass. ἱστημι
21.	(*lit.*)	'We were hoping that He was the one about to ransom Israel… He (?) is spending this third day from which these things happened.'
23.	εὑρουσαι	f. aor. part. εὑρισκω
23.	ἐωρακεναι	perf. infin. ὁραω for indirect statement
26.	παθειν	aor. infin. πασχω
28.	προσποιεομαι	I pretend
31.	διηνοιχθησαν	aor. pass. διανοιγω I open
33.	ἀθροιζω	I gather, collect
34.	ὡφθη	aor. pass. ὁραω
37.	πτοεω	I scare, strike panic
40.	ἐχοντα	acc. sing. pres. part.

34. The Nativity According to Matthew (1:18–2:23)

Basic Words

βουλομαι	I desire, wish, will (dist. from βουλευομαι I deliberate)
μικρος, -α, -ον	small, little [*microscope*]
ἐλαχιστος, -η, -ον	smallest, least
ἡγεομαι	I lead; I think (see GV)
ἡγεμων, -ονος	governor [*hegemony*]
κἀγω (και ἐγω)	and I, even I, I also
ἐπανω (adv. and prep. w. gen.)	above
προσφερω (see φερω)	I bring to, lead to; I offer (gifts, sacrifices etc.)
φευγω (2 aor. ἐφυγον)	I flee; I escape [via Latin *fugitive*]
ἀντι (prep. w. gen)	instead of, in return/ exchange for

General Notes

18.	μνηστευθεισης	aor. pass. part. f., incorrect gen. abs.
18.	ἐν γαστρι ἐχουσα	having-in-belly: being pregnant
20.	γεννηθεν	neut. aor. pass. part. γενναω
21.	τικτω, τεξομαι, ἐτεκον	
22.	ῥηθεν	neut. aor. pass. part. λεγω
1.	γεννηθεντος	aor. pass. part.; correct gen. abs.
2.	τεχθεις	aor. pass. part. τικτω
3.	ἐταραχθη	aor. pass. indic. ταρασσω
6.	ἐξελευσεται	fut. ἐξερχομαι
9.	ἐσταθη	aor. pass. indic. ἱστημι
10.	ἐχαρησαν χαραν	'cognate accusative'
11.	πεσοντες	aor. part. πιπτω
13.	ἰσθι	imper. εἰμι 'be!'
13.	εἰπω	aor. subj. λεγω for indef. fut.
20.	τεθνηκασιν	perf. ἀποθνησκω

35. The Agony, Arrest, and Trial of Jesus before Caiaphas (Mark 14:32–65)

Basic Words

παρερχομαι	I pass by (person and things); (fig.) I pass away, perish
μαχαιρα	a (short) sword
φιλεω	I love (of friendship); here, 'I kiss' [*philanthropy*]
ἐπιβαλλω	I throw, place, lay upon
καταλειπω (2 aor. – ἐλιπον)	I leave behind; I desert, abandon
ἐσω	(advbs.) within, inside (w. vbs. of rest or motion)
ἐσωθεν	(from) within, (from) inside
ὑπηρετης	servant, attendant, minister, officer (acc. to context)
ψευδομαι	I lie
ψευδος, -ους, το	an untruth
ψευδ-	false-
καταλυω	I break up, destroy (lit. and fig.)
βλασφημια	impious language, blasphemy; slander, abuse
προφητευω	I declare God's will, prophesy (not necessarily prediction)

General Notes

37.	μια	f. εἰς one
40.	pres. part. pass.	καταβαρυνω
41.	ἀπεχει	perhaps 'He (Judas) has received payment.'
42.	ἀγωμεν	intrans. subj. 'Let's go'
47.	παρεστηκοτων	intr. perf. part. παριστημι
49.	ἠμην	New Testament form 'I was' = ἠν
51.	περιβεβλημενος	perf. pass. part. περιβαλλω
55.	εἰς το	w. infin. mostly w. final force
62.	ὀψεσθε	fut. ὀραω
63.	διαρηξας	aor. part. διαρρησσω

36. Simon Magus and The Ethiopian Eunuch (Acts 8:4–40)

Basic Words

προσεχω	I attend to, turn mind to (understand τον νουν – see GV)
μονον (adv.)	alone, only
ἀργυριον	silver; money; silver coin [via Latin, *Argentina*]
δεομαι	I request, beg; I pray (Lucan) (dist. from δεω)
ἀρα (sometimes w. οὐν)	(so) then, therefore
ὑπερ	(prep. w. gen. more common) for, on behalf of; for sake of (w. acc.) over, beyond (indicating excess) (*hypercritical*)
κρισις, -εως, ἡ	decision, judgement (*crisis*)
ἀρπαζω	I seize, snatch, plunder (*harpy; harpoon?*)

General Notes

7.	βοωντα	n. pl. pres. part. βοαω
7.	παραλελυμενοι	perf. part. pass. παραλυω
9.	προϋπαρχω	I am previously
9.		lit. 'saying himself to be someone great'
11.	δια το	goes w. ἐξεστακεναι perf. infin., 'the having amazed'
16.	ἐπιπεπτωκος	n. perf. part ἐπιπιπτω
16.	βεβαπτισμενοι	ὑπηρχον periphrastic plup. pass.
19.	ἐπιθω	aor. subj. ἐπιτιθημι
20.	εἰη	optative εἰμι, for a wish
24.	εἰρηκατε	perf. λεγω
27.	ἐληλυθει	pluperfect ἐρχομαι
27.	προσκυνησων	fut. part., w. final force
30.	προσδραμων	aor. part. προστρεχω
30.	ἀρα	expects 'No'
32.	ἠχθη	aor. pass. ἀγω
33.	ἠρθη	aor. pass. αἰρω
38.	στηναι	2 aor. infin. ἱστημι

37. The Feet Washing (John 13:1–12)

Basic Words

ἑορτη	feast, festival
μεταβαινω (2 aor. – εβην)	I pass over; I withdraw, leave
τελος, – ους, το	end, result, fulfilment [*teleology*]
ἀρτι (adv.)	now, just now
κεφαλη	the head (lit. and fig.) [*encephalitis; cephalopod*]
καθαρος, -α, -ον	clean, pure [*Katharine; cathartic*]
ἀναπιπτω, (2 aor. ἀνεπεσον) ἀνακειμαι, ἀνακλινομαι	I recline at table

General Notes

1.	εἰδως	'pres.' part. οἰδα
2.	βεβληκοτος	perf. part. βαλλω, gen. abs.
2.	παραδοι	optative, for final clause
4.	διεζωσεν	aor. διαζωννυμι
7.	γνωσῃ	fut. γινωσκω
10.	λελουμενος	perf. pass. part. λουω

38. Gabriel and Zechariah (Luke 1:5–25)

Basic Words

ἐντολη	commandment, precept (see GV)
θυσια	sacrifice, offering
θυσιαστηριον	altar
θυω	I sacrifice, kill
ἀγαλλιασις, -εως, ἡ	ecstatic joy, delight
ἀγαλλιαω	I rejoice intensely, exult
κοιλια	belly, womb (general term) [*coeliac*]
ἐπιστρεφω (here trans.) (mostly intr.)	I turn; I turn (myself), I return (dist. ἐπιτρεπω)
μην, -ος, ὁ	month [*menopause*]

117

General Notes

6.	δικαιωμασιν	dat. pl. δικαιωμα
7.	προβεβηκοτες	perf. part. προβαινω
9.	ἐλαχε	from λαγχανω I obtain my turn
11.	ὠφθη	aor. pass. ὁραω
12.	ἐπεπεσεν	2 aor. ἐπιπιπτω
17.	προελευσεται	fut. προερχομαι
17.	κατεσκευασμενον	perf. pass. part. κατασκευαζω
19.	ἀπεσταλην	aor. pass. ἀποστελλω
20.	ἐση	fut. εἰμι
22.	ἑωρακεν	perf. act. ὁραω
25.	ἀφελειν	aor. infin. ἀφαιρεω

39. The Nativity According to Luke (2:1–40)

Basic Words

οἰκουμενη	the inhabited world (see GV) [*ecumenical*]
εἰρηνη	peace (Lucan) [*Irene*]
περιτεμνω	I cut around, circumcise
ἀναστασις, -εως, ἡ	a rising again, resurrection [*Anastasia*]
ἑπτα	seven [*heptagon*]
τελεω	I end, finish; I fulfil
αὐξανω (mostly intr.)	I grow, increase [*auxiliary*, via Latin *augment*]

General Notes

5.	οὔσῃ	f. dat. pres. part. εἰμι
6.	τεκειν	aor. infin. τικτω
11.	ἐτεχθη	aor. pass. τικτω
16.	ἀνευραν	aor. ἀνευρισκω
21.	κληθεν	aor. part. pass. n. καλεω
21.	συλλημφθηναι	aor. infin. pass. συλλαμβανω
24.	εἰρημενον	aor. pass. part. n. λεγω
26.	ἦν... κεχρηματισμενον	plup. pass. χρηματιζω
26.	πριν... ἰδη	indef. 'until he should see'
34.	ἀντιλεγομενον	contradicted, disputed
35.	ἀποκαλυφθωσιν	aor. subj. pass. ἀποκαλυπτω
38.	ἐπιστασα	f. aor. part. ἐφιστημι

40. The Trial before Pilate and The Crucifixion (John 19:1–42)

Basic Words

ἀγω (2 aor. ἠγαγον)	I lead (away), bring, guide; I go (intr.) [*pedagogue*]
αἰτια	cause, reason; crime; accusation [*aetiology*]
ἀνω (advbs.)	above; upwards
ἀνωθεν	from above; from beginning
σχιζω	I tear, split, divide
σχισμα, -ατος, το	a tear, split, division [*schism*]
σκευος, -ους, το	a vessel, implement;
τα σκευη	utensils, property; (fig. of people)
ἐπιτρεπω	I allow, permit (dist. ἐπιστρεφω)
πρωτον (adv.)	first, at the first (mostly of time)

General Notes

25. εἰστηκεισαν   plup. ἰστημι, w. imperf. meaning
26. παρεστωτα   perf. part. παριστημι w. pres. meaning
29. προσηνεγκαν   aor. προσφερω
31. κατεαγωσιν   from καταγνυμι
31. ἀρθωσιν   pass. aor. subj. αἰρω
33. τεθνηκοτα   perf. part. acc. ἀποθνησκω
35. ἑωρακως   perf. act. part. ὁραω
38. κεκρυμμενος   perf. pass. part. κρυππω
41. ἠν τεθειμενος   periphrastic plup. τιθημι

41. The Divorce Question; The Rich Young Ruler (Matthew 19:1–22)

Basic Words

περαν (prep. w. gen.)	beyond, across;
το περαν	the other side, country beyond
βιβλιον, το, βιβλος, ἡ	document, papyrus roll, a 'book' [*bibliography*]
συμφερω συμφερει	(intr. and gen. impers.) it is an advantage, expedient
κλεπτης	a thief [*kleptomania*]
κλεπτω	I steal
λυπεω	I distress, grieve
λυπη	pain (body or mind), grief

General Notes

1.	μετηρεν	1 aor. μεταιρω
6.	συνεζευξεν	1 aor. συζευγνυμι
12.	οἱτινες	generic 'who'
13.	προσηνεχθησαν	aor. pass. προσφερω
16.	σχω	aor. subj. ἐχω
21.	ἐξεις	fut. indic. ἐχω
22.	ἠν ἐχων	periphrastic imperf., to emphasise continuous action

42. What Does Contaminate (Matthew 15:10–20)

Basic Words

κοινος, -η, -ον	common, shared; (Heb.) profane, unclean
κοινοω	I make unclean, profane
νοεω, κατανοεω	I understand, perceive; I think, consider
κἀκεινος, -η, -ο	and he (she, it); he (she, it) also

General Notes

13.	ἐκριζωθησεται	fut. pass. ἐκριζοω
14.	πεσουνται	fut. act. πιπτω
20.	το... φαγειν	infin. of ἐσθιω, as verbal noun 'eating'

43. Feeding the Four Thousand and the Lesson Afterwards (Mark 8:6–21)

Basic Words

εὐχαριστεω
: I give thanks, am thankful [*Eucharist*]

παρατιθημι
: I place beside, I serve; (mid.) I deposit with, I entrust to

οὐπω
: not yet

General Notes

10.	ἐμβας	aor. part. ἐμβαινω
12.	εἰ	definitely not (as if an oath)
12.	δοθησεται	fut. pass. διδωμι
14.	ἐπελαθοντο	aor. ἐπιλανθανομαι
17.	γνους	aor. part. γινωσκω
17.	πεπωρωμενην	perf. pass. part. πωροω

44. The Woman Caught in Adultery; Jesus on Judgement (John 7:53–8:20)

Basic Words

κατηγορεω	I accuse, charge [*category*] (before a judge or in general)
ἐπιμενω (w. dat.)	I stay on, still remain; I persist, continue in
κἀν (και ἀν)	and if, even if, at least
ὑμετερος, -α, -ον	your, yours
ἡμετερος, -α, -ον	our, ours

General Notes

3.	κατειλημμενην καταλαμβανω	perf. part. pass.
3.	στησαντες trans.	1 aor. part. ἱστημι
4.	κατεληφθη καταλαμβανω	aor. pass.
9.	κατελειφθη	aor. pass. καταλειπω
19.	ἀν	closed condition: 'you would know'
20.	ἐληλυθει	plup. ἐρχομαι

45. Miscellaneous (Luke 8:9–56)

Basic words

The Sower Parable Explanation

μεριμνα	worry, anxiety, care
μεριμναω	I am anxious; I care for

The Storm on the Lake

παυω	(mid. intr.)	I cease; [*pause*]
	(act. trans.)	I stop (rare)

The Gerasene Demoniac

δεσμος	a bond, chain
	(plur. usually n. δεσμα)

Jairus' Daughter

διατασσω	I arrange, appoint
	[cf. *tactics*]

General Notes

9.	ἐπηρωτων	imperf. ἐπερωταω
9.	εἰη	optative εἰμι sum, for indirect question
22.	ἀνηχθησαν	aor. mid. ἀναγω
24.	Ἐπιστατα	voc. ἐπιστατης (six times in Luke only)
46.	ἐξεληλυθυιαν	perf. part. act. fem. acc. sing. ἐξερχομαι

46. Diana of the Ephesians (Acts 19:23–34)

Basic Words

ἐργατης   field-labourer, workman

ἀπολογεομαι   I defend myself

ἀπολογια   defence [*apology*]

General Notes

26.	μετεστησεν	tr. 1 aor. μεθιστημι
30.	εἰων	imperf. ἐαω
31.	δουναι	aor. infin. διδωμι
32.	συνεληλυθεισαν	plup. συνερχομαι

PART THREE

170 words characteristic of the Epistles

1. To Thessalonica
(1 Thessalonians 1–10)

Basic Words

χαρις, -ιτος, ἡ	grace, favour, charm; gratitude, thanks [*Charis, Charissa*]
παντοτε (adv.)	always
προσευχη	prayer
μνημονευω	I remember [*mnemonic*]
κοπος	(weary) toil, labour; trouble
ἀγαπη	love, goodwill, esteem (see GV)
ὑπομονη	patience, endurance
ἐλπις, -ιδος, ἡ	hope (see G.V.)
εὐαγγελιον	good news, Gospel
θλιψις, -εως, ἡ	distress, trouble
τυπος	figure, image; pattern, model [*type*]
δουλευω	I am a slave, am subject to, serve (almost always w. dat.)
ὀργη	anger

General Notes

4. ἠγαπημενοι   perf. pass. part. ἀγαπαω

5. οἱοι ἐγενηθημεν what kind (of men) we became

7. and 8. ὡστε and infin. for consecutive or result clause
    (adverbial)

8. ἐξηχηται   from ἐξηχεω I sound out

8. ἐξεληλυθεν   perf. ἐξερχομαι

9. ζωντι   pres. part. ζαω, in dat. after δουλευω

2. The Catholic Epistle of John* (1 John 2:1–28)

Basic Words

ἁμαρτανω	(orig. I miss mark; I make a mistake) I sin
τελειοω	I complete, perfect
ὀφειλω	I owe;
(w. infin.)	I ought (see ὠφελεω)
ἀγαπητος, -η, -ον	loved, beloved (see GV)
σκανδαλον	stumbling-block, cause of offence [scandal]
ἰσχυρος, -α, -ον	strong, powerful
ἐπιθυμια	desire, longing; (mostly in bad sense) lust
σαρξ, σαρκος, ἡ	flesh; human frailty (see GV) [sarcasm; sarcophagus]
φανεροω	I make clear, visible [cf. theophany]
ἐπαγγελια	a promise

---

*While the term 'Pastoral' for the three Timothy and Titus Epistles only appears to date from the 18th century, the designation 'Catholic Epistles' goes back as far as A.D. 310 or even earlier.

It was first mentioned by Eusebius, Bishop of Caesarea, the 'Father of Church History'. As far as the Eastern Church was concerned, the seven letters are so called because they are not addressed to individual churches, but are general or universal (i.e., 'catholic'). In the West, it denoted 'authoritative' or 'canonical'.

ἐπαγγελλομαι	I promise
πλαναω (mostly fig.) (pass.)	(act.) I lead astray, deceive; I am led astray, err [*planet* – from lit. sense 'to wander']
αἰσχρος, -α, -ον	shameful
αἰσχυνη	shame
αἰσχυνομαι	I am ashamed
παρουσια	presence; (mostly) arrival, advent [*Parousia*]
δικαιοσυνη	righteousness, justice

General Notes

6.	put καθως ἐκεινος περιεπατησεν last in sentence	
13.	νενικηκατε	perf. νικαω I conquer
18.	γεγονασιν	perf. γινομαι
19.	μεμενηκεισαν	plup. μενω, the ἀν making whole sentence a 'closed' condition
24.	μενετω	3rd s. imp.
24.	μενειτε	fut. of 'liquid' vb. μενω
28.	σχωμεν	aor. subj. ἐχω, for final clause

3. To Philippi (Philippians 2:1–18)

Basic Words

παρακλησις, εως, ἡ	exhortation; consolation [*Paraclete*]
κοινωνια	partnership, fellowship; contribution
φρονεω	I think (of), am mindful of [cf. *phrenology*]
ταπεινος, η, -ον	low degree, humble
ταπεινοφροσυνη	humility
ταπεινοω	I humble, make low
μεχρι (prep. w. gen.) (rare as conj.)	as far as, until even to (chiefly of time); until
διο	therefore, on which account
χαριζομαι	I graciously give; I forgive
γλωσσα	tongue; a language; ecstatic utterance [*glossary; glossolalia*]
ὑπακουω	(I hearken to) I obey
σωτηρια	salvation, deliverance (sacred and secular) [*soteriology*]
ἐνεργεω (intr.) (tr.)	I am at work; I work, effect something (pass. w. non-personal subject) it is made to work

χωρις (prep. w. gen.)	apart from, without (see πλην)
καυχημα, -ατος, το	boasting, 'glorying' exultation (grounds)
καυχησις, -εως, ἡ	boasting, 'glorying', exultation (act)
κενος, -η, -ον	empty; vain, fruitless [*cenotaph; kenotic doctrine*]
τρεχω (2 aor. ἐδραμον)	I run [cf. *syndrome; dromedary*]
κοπιαω	I grow weary; I labour, toil

General Notes

2.	το αὐτο	the same thing
3. and 6.	ἡγεομαι	I think; (also) I lead
3.	ἑαυτων	genitive of comparison
6.	το εἰναι	infin. as verbal noun, 'being'
6.	ἰσα	n. pl. used as advb. 'equally'
8.	εὑρεθεις	aor. pass. part. εὑρισκω
10.	ἐπουρανιων, ἐπιγειων, καταχθονιων	gen. pl. n.
15.	διεστραμμενης	perf. part. pass. διαστρεφω

4. To Philemon

Basic Words

ἐπιγνωσις, -εως, ἡ	knowledge, discernment
παρακαλεω	I entreat, beg; I exhort; I comfort
ποτε (indef. temp. part.)	once, formerly, sometime
πότε (interrog. adv.)	when? (ω. ἑως) how long?
κατεχω	I hold fast, possess; I hold back, restrain
ἀναγκαζω	I compel
ἀναγκαιος, -α, -ον	necessary, essential
ἀναγκη	necessity, compulsion
μαλιστα	most of all, especially (superl. of unused μαλα)
κοινωνεω (mostly w. dat.)	I share in, have fellowship with
κοινωνος (adj. used as noun)	a sharer, partner
ἀδικεω (intr.) (tr.)	I act unjustly; I wrong, hurt
πειθω (tr.) (intr.) (mid. or pass.)	I urge; I trust (in); I am persuaded (see GV)
ὑπακουη	obedience
ἁμα (adv.)	at the same time, together
ἐλπιζω	I hope (for)
ἀσπαζομαι	I greet, salute

General Notes

8.   ἀνῆκει   (impers.) it is fitting, proper (here n. part.)

14.   lit.   'in order that your good thing might not be as by compulsion, but willingly.'

15.   ἀπεχῃς   here trans. 'you might have him...'

18.   ἐλλογαω   (here imp.) I reckon

19.   'lest I say to you that you owe-in-addition to me even yourself.'

20.   ὀναιμην   opt. mid. ὀνινημι
                         may I have profit/derive benefit

21.   πεποιθως   perf. act. part. πειθω

5. The Catholic Epistle of James (James 3:13–4:7)

Basic Words

ἀναστρεφομαι	I conduct myself, live
ἀναστροφη	behaviour, manner of life
πραΰς, -εια, -υ	gentle, meek
πραΰτης, ητος, ἡ	gentleness, meekness
ζηλος	enthusiasm; jealousy [*zeal*]
ζηλοω	I am eager; I am jealous
πραγμα, -ατος, το	deed, action (past); [*pragmatic*] matter, affair (present)
πραξις, -εως, ἡ	doing, action
εἰτα, ἐπειτα	then, thereafter, next
ἐλεος, -ους, το	(also m., ὁ) pity, mercy, compassion
ἐπιθυμεω	I desire, long for; I lust after, covet
διοτι	because, for
καθιστημι (tr.)	I set, establish, appoint (see ἱστημι)
ὑποτασσω (act.)	I subject;
(mid. and pass.)	I submit

General Notes

13.   δειξατω   1 aor. imp. δεικνυμι

2.   ἐπιτυχειν   2 aor. infin. ἐπιτυγχανω

2.   δια το...   lit. 'on account of the not asking'

3.   aor. subj. of δαπαναω for final clause

5.   'The spirit which He made to dwell in us – does it long towards envy?'

7.   ἀντιστητε   2 aor. imp. ἀνθιστημι

6. To Colossae (Colossians 3:5–13)

Basic Words

πορνεια	fornication
πορνη	prostitute [*pornography*]
πορνος	fornicator, male prostitute
ἀκαθαρσια	uncleanness, impurity
κακια	wickedness, malice
ἐνδυω (mostly mid.)	I put on, clothe; I clothe myself, dress
νεος, -α, -ον	new [*neolithic*] (properly re time – see καινος); young
εἰκων, -ονος, ἡ	image, likeness [*iconoclasm*]
κτιζω	I create, found, make
περιτομη	circumcision (see GV)
ἀκροβυστια	'uncircumcision'
ἐλευθερια	freedom, liberty
ἐλευθερος, -α, -ον	free
ἐκλεκτος, -η, -ον	selected, chosen out, elect [*eclectic*]
μακροθυμεω	I am long-tempered
μακροθυμια	patience, long-suffering

General Notes

8. ἀπόθεσθε   2 aor. mid. imp. ἀποτίθημι

9. aor. mid. part. ἀπεκδυω (in that,) having stripped off

10. pres. pass. part. ἀνακαινοω = νεον and ἀνθρωπον

11. ἐνι = ἐνεστι is in, can be (here neg.)

7. To Ephesus – An Encyclical Letter?[*]
(Ephesians 3:13–4:15)

Basic Words

πλουτος, ὁ and το	riches, wealth [*plutocrat*]
θεμελιος	foundation (stone) [*theme*]
θεμελιοω	I found
γνωσις, -εως, ἡ	knowledge [*Gnostic*]
πληρωμα, -ατος, το	fullness, complement
ἀξιοω	I treat as worthy
ἀξιως	worthily [cf. *axiom*]
κλησις, -εως, ἡ	calling, invitation
κγητος, -η, -ον	called, invited
σπουδαζω	I hasten; I am eager
σπουδη	haste; eagerness
διακονια	service, ministration [*diaconate*]
τελειος, -α, -ον	complete, perfect
διδασκαλια	teaching, instruction
πλανη	a wandering, error [*planet*]
πλανος, -ον	deceiving; a deceiver

---

[*]There are at least three reasons to suggest that Ephesians was a letter for circulation between churches. See commentaries.

General Notes

16.	δῷ	aor. subj. διδωμι after ἱνα
17.	perf. pass. parts.	ῥιζοω and θεμελιοω
19.	γνωναι	aor. infin. γινωσκω
19.	f. pres. part.	ὑπερβαλλω = ἀγαπην
1.	ἐκληθητε	aor. pass. καλεω
5.	three genders of εἰς one	
7.	ἐδοθη	aor. pass. διδωμι
8.	Ἀναβας	2 aor. part. ἀναβαινω
14.	ὡμεν	pres. subj. εἰμι sum after ἱνα
15.	aor. subj.	αὐξανω, following ἱνα (at some distance)

8. To Timothy – A Pastoral Letter*
(1 Timothy 1:12–2:15)

Basic Words

πιστος, -η, -ον	faithful, believing (see GV)
προτερον	formerly, previously
ἐλεεω	I pity, show mercy/compassion
ἀγνοεω	I do not know, am ignorant of
ἀπιστεω	I disbelieve, am unfaithful
ἀπιστια	unbelief
ἀπιστος, -ον	unbelieving
τιμη	honour; price [*Timothy*]
προφητεια	declaration, 'prophecy' (see προφητης)
συνειδησις, -εως, ἡ	conscience
παιδευω	I instruct, educate; I chastise
δεησις, -εως, ἡ	begging, request, supplication
εὐχαριστια	thanksgiving, gratitude (*Eucharist*)
σωτηρ, -ηρος, ὁ	saviour, deliverer, preserver [*soteriology*]

---

*The designation 'Pastoral' for 1 and 2 Timothy and Titus dates, it seems, from the 18th century. They are so named because they deal with the 'shepherding' needed among existing churches, rather than the missionary stage in the development of the early church.

145

χρυσιον, χρυσος   gold [*chrysanthemum*; *Chrysostom*]

μανθανω (2 aor. ἐμαθον)   I learn [*mathematics*]

General Notes

12.	ἡγεομαι	I lead; also, I think (cf. Lat. *duco*)
12.	θεμενος	aor. mid. part. τιθημι
13.	ὀντα	acc. pres. part. εἰμι sum = με. Translate concessively: although being...
16.	'as an example of those about to believe'	
19.	aor. mid. part.	ἀπωθεω
6.	δους	aor. act. part. διδωμι
7.	ἐτεθην	aor. pass. τιθημι
9.	γυναικας	acc., following βουλομαι (at some distance)
14.	f. aor. pass. part. ἐξαπατεω	

9. The Catholic Epistle of Peter
(1 Peter 1:3–11)

Basic Words

κληρονομεω	I inherit, possess by inheritance
κληρονομια	inheritance, heritage
κληρονομος	an heir, inheritor
ἀποκαλυπτω (1 aor. ἀπεκαλυψα)	I reveal, disclose
πειρασμος	trial, testing; temptation
δοκιμαζω	I put to test, prove; I approve, think fit
ἐπαινεω	I praise
ἐπαινος	praise
ἀποκαλυψις, -εως, ἡ	revelation, unveiling [*Apocalypse*]
κομιζω (mid.)	I receive (back), recover
παθημα, -ατος, το	(an experience – see πασχω) suffering [*pathology*]

General Notes

3.   f. acc. pres. part. ζαω

4.   f. perf. pass. part. τηρεω = κληρονομιαν

7.   χρυσιου του ἀπολλυμενου genitive of comparison

11.   imperf. δηλοω 'continued to point out'

10. Το Galatia (Galatians 1:1–17)

Basic Words

ταχεως, ταχυ	quickly [*tachycardia*]
προλεγω	I tell/say beforehand; I declare plainly
γνωριζω	I make known
διωκω	I pursue (lit. and fig.); I persecute
γενος, -ους, το	family, offspring; race; sort, kind [via Latin, *generic*]
περισσος, -η, -ον	exceeding, excessive; uncommon, superior
περισσοτερως	more exceedingly, more abundantly
εὐδοκεω	I think it good, decide...; I am well-pleased (Biblical)

General Notes

4. ἐξεληται   aor. subj. mid. ἐξαιρεω

4. ἐνεστωτος   perf. part. ἐνιστημι

7. εἰ μη   only

8. παρα   w. acc. against

10. ἀν and imperfects, for 'closed condition' in pres. time

12. παρα   w. gen. from

15. and 16.   'when He who separated ...was
                  pleased to reveal... I did not con-
                  sult...' (main vb. προσαντιθημι)

11. The Apocalypse (Revelation 17:1–18)

Basic Words

κριμα, -ατος, το	judgement, verdict; condemnation
μυστηριον	a secret, mystery
μαρτυς, -υρος	a witness; a martyr
ἀπωλεια	destruction, loss; perdition
παρειμι	I am present, at hand (mostly of persons); I have come, arrived
νους, νοος, ὁ	mind, reason, intellect [slang *nous*]
γυμνος, -η, -ον	naked, ill-clad (usually w. under-garment) [*gymnasium*]
καιω	I ignite, burn [*caustic*]
κατακαιω	I burn down

General Notes

1. δειξω   fut. δεικνυμι

3. ἀπηνεγκεν   2 aor. ἀποφερω

4. perf. pass. part. περιβαλλω

4. as above for χρυσοω (lit. 'gilded with gold')

5. as above for γραφω

7. ἐρω fut. λεγω

8. lit. 'was, and is not, and shall ascend/be present,' i.e., respite from the Beast – at the moment.

10. indef. 'whenever he does come'

16. ἠρημωμενην f. perf. pass. part. ἐρημοω

16. φαγονται   fut. ἐσθιω

17. fut. pass. τελεω

12. The Second Letter to Corinth (2 Corinthians 5:1–21)

(RV or RSV crib recommended)

Basic Words

βαρεω	I weigh down
βαρος, -εος, το	weight, burden
βαρυς, -εια, -υ	heavy [*barytone; barathea?*]
εἰτε	and if;
εἰτε… εἰτε	whether… or
καυχαομαι	I boast, 'glory in', exult
κτισις, -εως, ἡ	creating, creation, creature
λογιζομαι	I reckon up, count; I consider, suppose
παραπτωμα, -ατος, το	(a falling-beside) lapse, trespass

General Notes

4. καταποθῇ   aor. subj. pass. καταπινω

5. δους   pres. part. act. διδωμι

16. ὡστε and *indic.* and so, consequently

18. δοντος as v.5

19. θεμενος   aor. mid. part. τιθημι

20. Θεου παρακαλουντος, ὡς and gen. abs.

21. γνοντα acc. aor. part. γινωσκω

13. The Letter to the Hebrews
(Hebrews 11:7–40)

Basic Words

κατακρινω	I condemn, give judgement against
ἀλλοτριος, -α, -ον	belonging to another; foreign, strange
ἐπει (conj.)	since, because; otherwise, else; introducing a question
ὀνειδιζω	I reproach
ὀνειδισμος	a rebuke
ἀπειθεια	disobedience
ἀπειθεω	I disobey; (prob.) I disbelieve
ἀπειθης, -ες	disobedient (basically 'unpersuasion')
ἀσθενεια	(not-strength) weakness; illness [neurasthenia]
τυγχανω (2. aor. ἐτυχον)	
(w. gen.)	I obtain, reach;
(abs.)	I chance, happen
ὑστερεω	I am in want, come short (of)
ὑστερημα, -ατος, το	the lacking, poverty

General Notes

11.	και	poss. concessive, 'although'
12.		perhaps 'from one sexually dead'
15.		closed condition w. ἄν: 'if… they *would* have had…'
17.	προσενηνοχεν	perf. of προσφερω, translate as if aor.
23.	ἐκρυβη	aor. pass. κρυπτω
25.	ἑλομενος	aor. mid. part. αἱρεω
26.	των θησαυρων	gen. of comp. 'than'; alternative construction to ἤ (than) in v.25.
34.	ἐσβεσαν	1 aor. σβεννυμι
40.	Θεου… προβλεψαμενου	gen. abs.

14. First Letter to Corinth (1 Corinthians 6:1–11)

Basic Words

τολμαω (usually w. infin.)	I dare, venture (to...)
ἀδικια	unrighteousness, iniquity
ἀδικος, -ον	unjust, unrighteous
ἐξουθενεω	(I set at nought) I despise, treat with contempt
διακρινω	I distinguish, discern; I decide, judge; (mid.) I doubt, hesitate
ἁγιαζω	(I make/treat as ἁγιος) I sanctify, consecrate; I purify
δικαιοω	I make/declare righteous, justify

General Notes

1. κρινω   mid. I go to law

2. κρινουσιν   fut. liquid vb.;

2. 'unworthy of the lowest courts'

3. μητιγε βιωτικα 'much more secular matters'

4. Perhaps 'If you (must) have secular courts, why make those sit who are despised in the church?' – i.e., pagan judges.

5. ἐνι   is in, can be

5. ἀνα μεσον   between

6. as for v.1

15. To Rome (Romans 1:8–19)

Basic Words

λατρευω	I serve, worship [*idolatry*]
πως	in some/any way, at all (indef. enclitic, much less freq. than πως;)
χαρισμα, -ατος, το	a gracious gift, spiritual endowment [*charismatic*]
πνευματικος, -η, -ον	spiritual (persons and things)
στηριζω	I confirm, strengthen
πολλακις (adv.)	often, frequently
φανερος, -α, -ον	clear, visible, 'open'

General Notes

10. fut. εὐοδοομαι I have a good journey – i.e., I prosper, succeed

11. aor. subj. μεταδιδωμι

11. aor. pass. infin. στηριζω

12. 'to be encouraged – together in you through one another's faith, both yours and mine.'

13. προεθεμην   2 aor. mid. προτιθημι

13. σχω   aor. subj. ἐχω

13. και   (twice) also, even

16. Christ Crucified
(1 Corinthians 1:18–31)

Basic Words

ἀθετεω   I set aside; I nullify; I reject

ἀσθενης, -ες   (not-strong)
                        weak, feeble; ill (morally and
                        spiritually, as well as physically)

καταργεω   I annul, abolish (lit. I make
                        idle)

General Notes

19.   ἀπολω   fut. of ἀπολλυμι

21.   'For since, in the wisdom of God, the world through
      (its) "wisdom" did not know God, God was pleased
      to…'

27.   ἐξελεξατο   aor. ἐκλεγομαι

29.   ὁπως ≡ ἱνα in order that (final); probably used for
      variety

17. No Extravagant Oaths (James 5:11–12)

Basic Words

ὑπομενω	I bear patiently, endure
ὀμνυμι, ὀμνυω	(1 aor. ὤμοσα) I swear, take an oath
μητε μητε... μητε	neither, nor; neither... nor

General Notes

12.	ἤτω =	ἐστω, imper. εἰμι
12.	πεσητε	aor. subj. πιπτω

18. Spirit, Not Letter (2 Corinthians 3:1–9)

Basic Words

ἐπιστολη a letter [*epistle*]

διακονος servant, attendant, minister; deacon [*diaconate*]

διαθηκη agreement, covenant; a will, testament

περισσευω (intr.) I overflow, abound; I excel
(tr.) I cause to exceed/ abound

General Notes

1. μη expects answer 'No'.

3. διακονηθεισα f. aor. pass. part.

3. πλαξιν dat. pl. πλαξ, πλακτος

7. lit. '…(so that the sons of Israel not to be able to gaze into the face of Moses, owing to the fading glory of his face)…'

19. General Precepts (Hebrews 13:5–9)

Basic Words

τροπος	manner, way [*tropic*; *heliotrope*]
ὠφελεω	I help, benefit [*Ophelia* – coined 1504?] (dist. fr. ὀφειλω I owe, ought)

General Notes

5.	παρουσιν	dat. pl. part. παρειμι
5.	ἀνω	aor. subj. ἀνιημι after οὐ μη, for strong future negative assertion
9.		'for it is good for the heart to be stabilised by grace, not by "food", those who lived [lit. *walked*] in which were not benefited.'

20. The Results of Saving Grace (Titus 2:11–15)

Basic Words

ἀνομια	lawlessness
ἀνομος, -ον	lawless
ἐλεγχω	I reprove; I expose

General Notes

11. ἐπεφανη — aor. ἐπιφαινω, w. meaning in pass. I appear, show myself

12. ζησωμεν — aor. subj. ζαω, after ἱνα

21. Christ's Fools (1 Corinthians 4:9–10)

Basic Words

φρονιμος, -ον	sensible, prudent
ἀτιμαζω	I dishonour, insult
ἀτιμια	dishonour, disgrace
ἀτιμος, -ον	unhonoured, dishonoured

General Notes

ἀπεδειξεν	9. aor. act. ἀποδεικνυμι, I exhibit, display

22. Adoration of the Lamb
(Revelation 5:11–14)

Basic Words

εὐλογια	(a) blessing [*eulogy*]
κρατος, -ους, το	power, might; dominion, rule [*democratic*]

General Notes

11. μυριας   ten thousand [*myriad*]
    χιλιας   a thousand

12. ἐσφαγμενον   n. perf. part. pass. σφαζω

PART FOUR
General Vocabulary

A Note on Selection

The general rule is that a word occurring at least ten times is considered to be worth including in the list. This, however, needs to be qualified in a number of respects. The same word coming several times in the same chapter is only counted as one; words found two, three, or even four times in parallel narratives in the Synoptists and in the Fourth Gospel are still only counted once. Both these norms may seem unnecessarily severe, but at least they do ensure that ultimately only the most important words are included. An example of these two rules is the verb σπειρω (I sow). It has a gross total of forty-seven, but finally is reduced to a nett nine occurrences. This, of course, is an extreme case, and the verb has been included with its cognate σπερμα (seed). Indeed, many words such as ὑψοω (I raise to a height) and σχιζω (I tear) are not by themselves numerous enough, but they become sufficiently common when combined with their cognates. Similarly, compound and simple verbs can be put together such as νοεω and κατανοεω (I understand) and ἐρωταω and ἐπερωταω (I ask a question) when the meaning is almost the same. Occasionally two quite different words can be combined, such as πιπρασκω and πωλεω (I sell). So much for frequency.

Secondly, there is the question of distribution. If a word is of fairly common occurrence in one particular book, or in a few books, and is rarely come upon elsewhere, it is not worth learning especially. Should students be reading that book, they will very soon come across it in any case. Such words can sometimes be slipped conveniently into the definition of their more frequent cognates, as before. Examples of these ill-distributed words are βροντη (thunder – Revelation), κελευω (I command – Matthew and Acts), and ἀτενιζω, πληθος, παραχρημα (I gaze, crowd, immediately – all Lucan favourites, strongly illustrating incidentally the unity of authorship of the Third Gospel and Acts). If there is a doubt, the deciding factor is whether the word is found chiefly in the Gospels and Acts rather than in the Epistles.

Thirdly, any word which only just satisfies frequency and distribution requirements, but which has a number of meanings, perhaps in various moods, is omitted in the interests of simplicity. Instances of such complex words are συνεχω (I hold together), ἀπεχω (I am distant from), and a number of verbs ending in μι.

A

α, as a prefix, has two (perhaps three) uses: ἀ (ἀν before a vowel) negative; ἀ copulative (indicating community and fellowship); ἀ intensive (doubted or denied by many scholars).

ἀγαθος, -η, -ον	good (in essence – whether apparent or not) [*Agatha*]
το ἀγαθον	'the good' (used abstractly)
ἀγαλλιασις, -εως, ἡ	ecstatic joy, delight
ἀγαλλιαω	I rejoice intensely, exult
ἀγαπαω	I love (never sexual; mostly of mutual love between God and us, and between us and our fellows)
ἀγαπη	love, goodwill, esteem (In Biblical and ecclesiastical books only. In LXX generally sexual. ἀγαπη is love of the will rather than emotions – 'the love of the unlovable.' Cf. 'charity' in AV period.)
ἀγαπητος, -η, -ον	loved, beloved (Used as Messianic title and between Christians. In classical Greek ἀγαπαω meant 'to be content' and was applied to an 'only' child. In LXX ἀγαπητος had this μονογενης sense and it is possible that it has this meaning in the New Testament also.)
ἀγγελος	a messenger, an angel
ἀγιαζω	(I make/treat as ἀγιος) I sanctify, consecrate; I purify

171

ἅγιος, -α, -ον	set-apart, holy, sacred; οἱ ἁγ. saints, Christians [*hagiology*]
ἀγνοεω	I do not know, am ignorant of [*agnostic* – coined 1870]
ἀγοραζω	I buy (ἀγορα market-place)
ἀγρος	a field; the country; a piece of ground; (pl.) lands, farms [cf. Lat. 'ager'; *agriculture*]
ἀγω (2 aor. ἠγαγον)	I lead (away), bring, guide; [*pedagogue*]
(intr.)	I go
ἀδελφη	a sister; a Christian woman
ἀδελφος	brother (literal), a neighbour, a fellow-national, or a fellow-Christian [*Philadelphia*]
ἀδικεω (intr.)	I act unjustly;
(tr.)	I wrong, hurt
ἀδικια	unrighteousness, iniquity
ἀδικος, -ον	unjust, unrighteous
ἀθετεω	I set aside; I nullify; I reject
αἱμα, -ατος, το	blood (in ordinary sense and several special ones) [*anaemic; haemorrhage*]
αἱρω (1 aor. ἠρα)	I raise; I carry; I take away
αἰσχρος, -α, -ον	shameful
αἰσχυνη	shame

αἰσχυνομαι, ἐπ.-	I am ashamed
αἰτεω (mid.)	I ask, request; I ask for myself (the vb. has at least five compounds)
αἰτια	cause, reason; crime; accusation [*aetiology*]
αἰων, -ωνος, ὁ	an age, time-cycle, eternity; the present age, an era; οἱ αἰ, the worlds, the universe [*aeon*]
αἰωνιος, -ον	age-long, eternal (without beginning and/or end)
ἀκαθαρσια	uncleanness, impurity
ἀκαθαρτος, -ον	unclean, impure (ceremonially and morally)
ἀκοη	hearing, ear; message, teaching; report, rumour
ἀκολουθεω (w. dat.)	I accompany, follow [*acolyte*] (replacing ἑπομαι, which is not in the New Testament)
ἀκουω (1 aor. ἠκουσα)	I hear, listen (when tr. it is, strictly speaking, w. acc. of thing and gen. of person) [*acoustics*]
ἀκροβυστια	(foreskin) uncircumcision
ἀληθεια	truth (in widest sense, both objective and subjective)
ἀληθης, -ες	true (*things*), truthful (*persons*)
ἀληθινος, -η, -ον	true, real, genuine (lit. 'made of truth')

ἀληθως (adv.)	truly, indeed, certainly
ἀλλα	but (± a previous negation) (dist. from ἀλλα other things)
ἀλληλους, -ων, -οις	(also f. and n.) one another, mutually (reciprocal pronoun, w. no nom.)
ἀλλος, -η, -ο	other, another (numerical, whereas ἑτερος denotes qualitative difference) [*allegory*]
ἀλλοτριος, -α, -ον	belonging to another; foreign, strange
ἁμα (adv.)	at the same time, together
ἁμαρτανω (2 aor. ἡμαρτον)	(orig. perhaps, I miss mark; I make a mistake) I sin
ἁμαρτια	sin (abstract, general, and particular)
ἁμαρτωλος, -ον	sinful; a sinner (adj. used as noun)
ἀμην (Heb.)	truly, verily, indeed, certainly (Gospels only); Amen! So let it be!
ἀν	an untranslatable conditional particle = 'under the circumstances', 'in that case', 'anyhow'. Its general effect is to make a statement *contingent*, which would otherwise be definite. Thus w. subj. ἑως ἀν until such time as; ὁστις ἀν whosoever... Used w. imp. or aor. indic. in apodosis of conditional sentence (the 'then' clause): ἀν... μετενοησαν they *would have* repented. Verb alone – they repented. Luke (Gospel and

Acts) uses ἀν w. optative mood a
dozen times.

ἀναβαινω, – βησομαι, – εβην, – βεβηκα
(persons)   I go up, ascend;
(things)   I rise, spring up

ἀναβλεπω   I look up; I recover sight

ἀναγγελλω (1 aor. – ηγγειλα) I report, I announce

ἀναγινωσκω (2 aor. ἀνεγνων) I read

ἀναγκαζω   I compel

ἀναγκαιος, -α, -ον   necessary

ἀναγκη   necessity; compulsion

ἀναγω (see ἀγω)   I lead/bring up;
    (mid.)   I put to sea (chiefly Acts)

ἀνακειμαι, ἀνακλινομαι, ἀναπιπτω I recline at table

ἀναστασις, -εως, ἡ   a rising again, resurrection
             [*Anastasia*]

ἀναστρεφομαι   I conduct myself, live

ἀναστροφη   behaviour, manner of life

ἀνεμος   wind [*anemone; anemometer*]

ἀνηρ, ἀνδρος (Lat. *vir*) a man; a husband; [*polyandry*]
(voc. pl.)   'Gentlemen…'

ἀνθρωπος (Lat. *homo*) a human being, man; [*anthropology*]
             someone (definite and indefinite)

ἀνιστημι   I rise; (intr. in mid. and 2 aor. act.
             -εστην);
             I raise, set up (less often; tr. in fut.
             -στησω and 1 aor. -εστησα)

175

ἀνοιγω (1 aor. ἠνοιξα)	I open
ἀνομια	lawlessness
ἀνομος, -ον	lawless, wicked
ἀντι (prep. w. gen.)	instead of, in return/exchange for
ἀνω (advs.)	above; upwards
ἀνωθεν	from above; from beginning, again
ἀξιος, -α, -ον	worthy, deserving; suitable (of things) (often w. gen.) [*axiom*]
ἀξιοω	I treat as worthy
ἀξιως	worthily
ἀπαγγελλω (1 aor. -ηγγειλα)	I report; I announce
ἀπας, -ασα, -αν	quite all, the whole (strengthened πας. Lucan)
ἀπειθεια	disobedience
ἀπειθεω	I disobey (poss. I disbelieve – basic meaning 'unpersuasion')
ἀπειθης, -ες	disobedient
ἀπερχομαι (2 aor. -ηλθον)	I go away from, leave
ἀπιστεω	I disbelieve, am unfaithful
ἀπιστια	unbelief
ἀπιστος, -ον	unbelieving
ἀπο (prep. w. gen.)	from, away from (exterior). It denotes departure, partitive sense, riddance, distance, time, or-

176

der, origin, instrument, or agent (e.g., 'by'), etc. [*apostasy*].

ἀποδιδωμι (see διδωμι) I give back, restore; I render as due

ἀποθνησκω
(2. aor. ἀπεθανον)
I die (natural, violent and spiritual)

ἀποκαλυπω
(see 1 aor ἀπεκαλυψα)
I reveal, disclose

ἀποκαλυψις, -εως, ἡ revelation, unveiling [*apocalypse*]

ἀποκρινομαι
(1 aor. pass. ἀπεκριθην)
I answer, reply
(often used redundantly); I begin to speak (the latter two are Hebraistic)

ἀποκτεινω
(1 aor. ἀπεκτεινα)
I kill

ἀπολλυμι
(1 aor ἀπωλεσα)
(mid.)
I destroy completely;
I lose utterly;
I perish, am lost [*Apollyon; Apollo*]

ἀπολογεομαι I defend myself

ἀπολογια defence [*apology*]

ἀπολυω (see λυο) I set free, release;
I let go, dismiss, divorce

ἀποστελλω
(1 aor. – εστειλα)
I send away, commission

ἀποστολος a messenger, delegate; an Apostle (the Twelve and perhaps half-a-dozen others)

ἀπτομαι
(1 aor. ἡψαμην)
(w. gen.) I touch, take hold of (the active ἀπτω I light – Lucan)

177

ἀπωλεια	destruction, loss; perdition [cf. *Apollyon, Apollo*]
ἀρα	(inferential particle, sometimes w. οὖν) (so) then, therefore
ἀργυριον	silver; money; silver coin [cf. *Argentine*]
ἀρνεομαι, ἀπαρν. (1 aor. ἠρνησαμην)	I deny; I disown, repudiate
ἁρπαζω	I seize, snatch, plunder [*harpy; harpoon?*]
ἀρτι (adv.)	now, just now
ἀρτος	bread, a loaf; food
ἀρχη	beginning, origin; sovereignty, rule [*archaeology; monarchy*]
ἀρχιερευς, -εως	high-priest (e.g., Caiaphas and Annas); (pl.) ex-high-priests and members of such families; chief priest (heads of the twenty-four divisions, although this is possibly doubtful)
ἀρχομαι	I begin (often used periphrastically (1 aor. ἠρξαμην) w. infin. – instead of imp. or aor. alone – probably representing Aramaic originals: e. g., ἠρξατο διδασκειν – He began to teach.)
ἀρχων, -οντος	ruler, governor (in wide sense: Sanhedrin members, synagogue rulers, judges and magistrates etc.) [*monarch*]

ἀσθενεια	(not-strength) weakness; illness [*neurasthenia*]
ἀσθενεω	(not-strong) I am weak; I am sick [*neurasthenic*]
ἀσθενης, -ες	(not-strong) weak, feeble; ill (morally and spiritually, as well as physically)
ἀσπαζομαι	I greet, salute
ἀτιμαζω	I dishonour, insult
ἀτιμια	dishonour, disgrace
ἀτιμος, -ον	unhonoured, dishonoured
αὐξανω	I grow, increase (in New Testament mostly intr., seldom tr., sometimes pass.) [*auxiliary*; *augment.*, via Latin]
αὐτος, αὐτη, αὐτο	(emphatic pron.) self; [*automatic*] he, she, it; they (in gen. = his, her, its; their);
ὁ, ἡ, το αὐτ.	the same
ἀφεσις, -εως, ἡ	(from ἀφιημι) remission, forgiveness
ἀφιημι (1 aor. ἀφηκα)	I send away; I let go; I remit, forgive; I leave alone, neglect; I allow, permit
ἀχρι (prep. w. gen.) (conj. ± οὐ)	until, unto (time and space); until (w. subj. or indic.)

B

βαλλω, βαλω, ἐβαλον, I throw; I put, place [*ballistics*]
βεβληκα, βεβλημαι, ἐβληθην

βαπτιζω	(I dip, submerge) I baptise
βαπτισμα, -ατος, το	immersion, baptism
βαρεω	I weigh down
βαρος, -εος, το	weight, burden
βαρυς, -εια, -υ	heavy [*baritone; barathea?*]
βασιλεια	sovereignty, royal authority; a/the kingdom, realm
βασιλευς, -εως	a king [*Basil*]
βασταζω	I carry (off); I bear, endure
βιβλιον, το, βιβλος, ἡ	document, papyrus roll, a 'book' [*bibliography*]
βλασφημεω	I abuse, insult (God or man)
βλασφημια	impious language, blasphemy; slander, abuse
βλεπω	I see, look at; I perceive, discern; I consider, take heed
βουλομαι	I desire, wish, will (stronger than θελω) (distinguish from βουλευομαι I deliberate)

Γ

γαρ	for (main meaning; second word in a clause)
γε	indeed, really (emphatic particle, often too subtle to translate)
γενεα	a generation [*Genealogy*]
γενναω	I beget, bring forth; (pass.) I am born [*hydrogen*]
γενος, -ους, το	family, offspring; race; sort, kind [via Latin, *generic*]
γευομαι	I taste; (fig.) I experience
γη	the earth, soil, land [*Geology*]
γινομαι (2 aor. mid. ἐγενομην)	I come into being (persons, things and occurrences); I happen (events); I am made; I become
γινωσκω (2 aor. ἐγνων)	I am taking in knowledge, perceive; (past tenses) I know, realise
γλωσσα, -ης	tongue; a language; utterances in ecstasy [*glossary; glossolalia*]
γνωριζω	I make known
γνωσις, -εως, ἡ	knowledge [*Gnostic*]
γνωστος, -η, -ον	known; an acquaintance
γραμμα, -ατος, το	letter of alphabet, writings, document

γραμματευς, -εως	scribe, teacher of the Law
γραφη	a writing; Scripture text; (pl.) Old Testament Scriptures
γραφω	I write [*telegraph*]
γρηγορεω	I am on the watch, alert [*Gregory*]
γυμνος, -η, -ον	naked, ill-clad (generally, wearing under-garment only) [*gymnastics*]
γυνη, γυναικος	a woman; wife (voc. γυναι, dat. pl. γυναιξι) [*gynaecology*]

Δ

δαιμονιον	an evil spirit, demon
δε	but, on the other hand; and (a weak adversative particle, generally placed second in its clause, and often answering μεν)
δεησις, -εως, ἡ	a begging, request, supplication
δει (imperf. ἐδει)	(impers.) it is necessary, one must
δεικνυμι (or δεικνυω), δειξω, ἐδειξα	I show, point out; I make known
δεξιος, -α, -ον	(on) the right hand, right [*dextrous*, via Latin]
δεομαι (dist. from δεω)	I request, beg; I pray (Lucan favourite)
δεσμιος, -α, -ον	(lit. captive, bound) a prisoner

δεσμος	(pl. usually n. δεσμα) bond, chain
δευρο, δευτε	(s. and pl. respectively; advs. used as imperatives) Here! Come!
δευτερος, -α, -ον	second; δευτερον adverbially: secondly, for second time [*Deuteronomy*]
δεχομαι	I receive, accept; I welcome
δεω	I bind, tie [*arthrodesis; diadem*]
δια (w. gen.)	through; [*diathermy*] throughout; by (place, time, means);
(w. acc.)	on account of, by reason of; signifying 'through' w. vbs.; as intensifying prefix; and with other meanings.
διαβολος	the Devil; a slanderer [*diabolic*]
διαθηκη	agreement, covenant; a will, testament
διακονεω	I wait at table, I serve (generally)
διακονια	service, ministration
διακονος	servant, attendant, minister; deacon [*diaconate*]
διακρινω	I distinguish, discern; I decide, judge; (mid.) I doubt, hesitate
διαλογιζομαι	I reason, consider
διαλογισμος	reasoning, deliberation [*dialogue*]
διατασσω	I arrange, appoint, give order [cf. *tactics*]

διδασκαλια	teaching, instruction, doctrine (Pastoral favourite)
διδασκαλος	a teacher
διδασκω, διδαξω, εδιδαξα, —, —, εδιδαχθην	I teach, give instruction
διδαχη	teaching, instruction, doctrine [*didactic*]
διδωμι, δωσω, εδωκα, δεδωκα, δεδομαι, εδοθην	I give (in numerous senses) [*antidote*]
διερχομαι (2 aor. διηλθον)	I go through, pass through (Lucan favourite)
δικαιος, -α, -ον	righteous, just (persons), right (things)
δικαιοσυνη	righteousness, justice
δικαιοω	I make/declare righteous, justify
διο	therefore, on which account
διοτι	because, for
διωκω	I pursue (lit. and fig.); I persecute
δοκεω	I suppose, think; I seem, am thought [*Docetism*]
δοκει (impers. w. dat.)	it seems
δοκιμαζω	I put to the test, prove; I approve, think fit
δοξα	(good) opinion, repute; honour, glory; visible glory [*paradox*]

184

δοξαζω	I praise, magnify; I glorify [*doxology*]
δουλευω	I am a slave, am subject to, serve (almost always w. dat.)
δουλος	slave, bondservant
δυναμαι	I am powerful able [*dynasty*]; I am able to, I can (w. infin.) (cf. ἰσχυω)
δυναμις, -εως, ἡ (pl.)	power, might, ability; [*dynamic*] powerful deeds, marvellous works
δυνατος, -η, -ον	powerful, strong; able to (w. infin.); possible (n. δυνατον)
δυο (dat. δυσι)	two [cf. Latin *dual*]
δωδεκα	(the) twelve (apostles) [*dodecagon*]
δωρον, το, δωρεα, ἡ	a gift, present[*Dorothy, Theodore*]
δωρεαν	freely, as a gift (adv. acc.)

E

ἐαν   if (w. subj. for conditions); from 2nd cent. BC used indefinitely within a clause, modifying ὁς, ὁσος κ.τ.λ. into 'whosoever' – as the Attic ἀν does.

ἑαυτου, -ης, -ου   (reflexive pron.) self, selves (for almost all persons and genders, s. and pl., according to context)

ἐγγιζω   I come near, approach

ἐγγυς   near (time and place)
(adv. and prep., mostly w. gen.)

ἐγειρω   I wake, arouse; I raise up

ἐγω, ἐμε, ἐμου, ἐμοι   (full forms) I, me, of me, to/for me (nom. for emphasis or contrast) [*egocentric*]

με, μου, μοι   (enclitic forms) used w. nouns, adjs., vbs., advs. where there is no emphasis

ἐθνος, -ους, το   people, race; τα ἐθνη nations, Gentiles [*ethnology, ethnic*]

εἰ   if (introducing clauses w. indic.); εἰ μη if not, unless, except; if, whether (in indirect and direct questions); indeed, assuredly (not) – in strong statements, oaths etc.

εἰκων, -ονος, ἡ   image, likeness [*iconoclasm*]

εἰμι, ἐσομαι, ἠν (imp.)   I am, exist (freq. in imperf. w. participles, used periphrastically)

εἰρηνη   peace (Lucan) [*Irene*]

εἰς (prep. w. acc.)   (place) into, to, towards;
(time) for, unto, until;
εἰς το w. infin. for purpose, result;
εἰς is sometimes weakened to ἐν = in (see lexicon for a host of meanings) [*eisegesis*]

εἰς, μια, ἐν
(ἑνος m. and n. gen.)   one [*henotheism*]

εἰτα, ἐπειτα   then, thereafter, next

εἰτε   and if

εἰτε... εἰτε   whether... or

ἐκ, ἐξ (before vowels)
(prep. w. gen.)   (of place) from out of, from, from among;
(of time) from, since;
frequently used of 'origin'*
[*exodus; ecstasy*]

ἐκαστος, -η, -ον   each, every (of more than two)

ἐκβαλλω   I throw out, expel, exorcise;
(in weaker sense) I take out, remove

ἐκει (adv.)   there; 'thither', there (w. vbs. of motion)

ἐκειθεν (adv.)   from there

---

*For a full list, see the Addendum on page 492 of G. Abbot-Smith's *Lexicon*.

ἐκεινος, -η, -ο	(demon. pron.) he, she, it, they (implying remoteness); (adj.) that, those
ἐκκλησια	(lit. 'a calling-out') an assembly, meeting; community, congregation, local church; the Church [*ecclesiastic*]
ἐκλεγομαι	I choose, pick out for myself
ἐκλεκτος, -η, -ον	selected, chosen out, elect [*eclectic*]
ἐκπορευοραι	I journey out; I come forth
ἐκχεω, ἐκχυνω	I pour out, shed, spill
ἐλαια	olive tree
ἐλαιον	olive oil
ἐλεγχω	I convict; I rebuke; I expose
ἐλεεω	I pity, show mercy/compassion
ἐλεος, -ους, το	(also m., ὁ) pity, mercy, compassion
ἐλευθερια	freedom, liberty
ἐλευθερος, -α, -ον	free
ἐλπιζω	I hope (for)
ἐλπις, -ιδος, ἡ	hope (Elpis – name of Herod's eighth wife?)
ἐμαυτον, -ου, -ῳ	(and f.) (reflexive and so no nom.) myself
ἐμος, -η, -ον	my, mine

ἔμπροσθεν	(adv., but mostly prep. w. gen.) before, in front (of), in presence of
ἐν (w. dat.)	in (the basic meaning); additional to 'place', it can have the sense of 'state or condition' (in a mystery), 'agent or instrument' (with water), and 'time' (in the day). [*enthusiast*]
ἐνδύω	I put on, clothe; (mostly mid.) I clothe myself, dress
ἕνεκεν (prep. w. gen.)	on account of, for the sake of
ἐνεργέω	(intr.) I am at work; (tr.) I work, effect something; (pass. w. non-personal subject) it is made to work, actuated
ἐντέλλομαι	I command, instruct
ἐντεῦθεν (adv.)	from here, 'hence'
ἐντολη	order, injunction (esp. religious precept or commandment)
ἐνώπιον	(used as prep. w. gen.) in presence of, before face of (Lucan and Revelation)
ἐξ	six [*hexagon*]
ἔξεστιν	it is permitted, lawful (impers.)
ἐξιστημι (tr.) (more often intr.)	I astonish, amaze; I am astonished; I am mad [*ecstatic*]
ἐξουθενέω	(I set at nought) I despise, treat with contempt

ἐξουσια	power, authority; (quasi-personally for angel or magistrate etc.) spiritual or earthly 'power'
ἐξω (adv.) (prep. w. gen.)	out, outside (sometimes w. article) out of
ἑορτη	feast, festival
ἐπαγγελια	a promise
ἐπαγγελλομαι	I promise
ἐπαινεω	I praise
ἐπαινος	praise
ἐπαιρω	I raise up, lift up
ἐπανω	(adv. and prep. w. gen.) above
ἐπαυριον, αὐριον	on the morrow, tomorrow (ἐχθες yesterday; σημερον today)
ἐπει (conj.)	since, because; otherwise, else; (for introducing a question)
ἐπι (prep.)	

	most often w. acc.	(place) on, upon, over (lit. and fig., and frequently after vbs. of motion); [*epidermis*] (time) during, as long as;
	w. gen.	(place) on, upon; at, by; in presence of; (time) in/at the time of;
	w. dat.	(lit.) on, upon (similar to acc. usage), at, by; (fig.) regarding the ground, reason etc.; over (w. vbs. of emotion).

There are a dozen other meanings for the dative alone, according to context.

ἐπιβαλλω	I throw, place, lay upon
ἐπιγινωσκω	I know accurately; I recognise, perceive; I discover
ἐπιγνωσις, -εως, ἡ	precise knowledge, discernment (mostly of religion and morals)
ἐπιθυμεω	I desire, long for; I lust after, covet
ἐπιθυμια	desire, longing (mostly in bad sense), lust
ἐπικαλεω	I surname, nickname; (mid.) I call upon, appeal to
ἐπιλαμβανομαι	I lay/take hold of (friendly or hostile)
ἐπιμενω (w. dat.)	I stay on, still remain; I persist, continue in
ἐπιστολη	a letter [*epistle*]
ἐπιστρεφω (mostly intr.) (tr.)	I turn (myself), I return; I turn
ἐπιτιθημι	I place/lay upon
ἐπιτιμαω (w. dat.)	I rebuke; (w. ἱνα) I warn, charge
ἐπιτρεπω	I allow, permit (dist. from ἐπιστρεφω)
ἑπτα	seven [*heptagon*]
ἐργαζομαι (mostly tr.) (intr.)	I produce by work, work out, perform; I am at work, I work

ἐργατης	field-labourer, workman
ἐργον	work, labour; (more often) action, deed [*energy*]
ἐρημος, -ον	(adj. used as fem. noun) desolate, lonely; the desert [*hermit*]
ἐρχομαι, ἐλευσομαι, ἠλθον, ἐληλυθα	I come; (rarely) I go (defective vb. – cf. our 'go' and 'went')
(εἰσερχομαι	I come/go into, I enter;)
(ἐξερχομαι	I come/go out of)
ἐρωταω, ἐπερωταω	I ask a question, I question; I request, beg (similar to αἰτεω)
ἐσθιω (2 aor. ἐφαγον)	I eat (tr. and intr.) [*phagocyte, sarcophagus*]
ἐσχατος, -η, -ον	last (mostly of time) [*eschatology*]
ἐσω	within, inside (w. vbs. of rest or motion)
(advs.)	
ἐσωθεν	(from) within, (from) inside
ἐτερος, -α, -ον	the other (second of a pair); the next; one's neighbour; another, other (of more than two); other, different (of quality) (Lucan) [*heterodox*]
ἐτι (adv.)	(time) still, (as) yet, even now; (degree) more, further, even, still
ἐτοιμαζω	I prepare, make ready
ἐτοιμος, -η, -ον	ready, prepared

ἔτος, -ους, το	a year [*Etesian wind*]; ἐνιαυτος (a cycle of time) a year
εὐαγγελιζω	(mostly mid., – ομαι) I proclaim good news; I preach the Gospel, good tidings (Lucan) [*evangelise*]
εὐαγγελιον	good news (of Messiah's Advent, Gospel and of the Kingdom)
εὐδοκεω	I think it good, decide…; I am well-pleased (Biblical usage)
εὐθεως, εὐθυς	immediately, at once (Marcan) (sometimes weakened to an inferential 'then', 'so then': e.g., in Mark 1)
εὐλογεω	(lit. I speak well) I bless; I praise
εὐλογια	(a) blessing [*eulogy*]
εὑρισκω (2 aor. εὑρον)	I find; I find out, discover I find for myself, obtain [*heuristic*]
εὐχαριστεω	I give thanks, am thankful
εὐχαριστια	thanksgiving, gratitude [*Eucharist*]
ἐχθρος, -α, -ον	(adj. hating, hostile, used often as a noun) enemy
ἐχω, ἑξω, εἰχον (imp.), ἐσχον, ἐσχηκα	I have, hold, possess;
(w. infin.)	I am able to…;
(w. adv.)	= εἰμι w. corresponding adj. (κακως ἐχειν to be ill)
(mid. – ομαι)	I hold on, cling to; I am next, near to (place and time)

ἑως (conj.)	until (for a fact in past time, w. indic.);
	(± οὐ or ὁτου, and followed by aorist subj., ± ἀν or ἐαν, to denote an indefinite time)
(prep. w. nouns in gen., advs. or other preps.)	(time) until, up to; (place) as far as, up to; (measure) as much as

Z

ζαω	I live
ζηλος	enthusiasm; jealousy [*zeal*]
ζηλοω	I am eager; I am jealous (of)
ζητεω, ἐπιζητεω	I search for, seek
ζωη	life (physical or spiritual) [*Zoë*; cf. *Zoology*]

H

ἡ	or (between words and sentences); than (in comparative sentences, w. same case after as before – the alternative construction to 'genitive of comparison')
ἡγεομαι	I lead; I guide, rule; I think, suppose
ἡγεμων, -ονος	governor [*hegemony*]

ἤδη	now, already
ἥκω (fut. ἥξω)	I have come, am present (perf. w. pres. meaning)
ἥλιος	the sun (± article) [*heliograph; heliotrope*]
ἡμεις, ἡμας, ἡμων, ἡμιν	we, us (declined pl. of ἐγω, I); (the nom. for emphasis or contrast)
ἡμερα	day (opp. to night); ' twenty-four hours'; Last Day; time in general [*ephemeral*]

Θ

θαλασσα, -ης	sea [*thalassic*]
θανατος	death [*euthanasia*]
θαυμαζω (tr.)	I am astonished, surprised; I wonder at, admire
θεαομαι	I look at, contemplate [*theatre*]
θελημα, -ατος, το	the will [*monothelite*]
θελω, ἐθελω ού θελω (1 aor. ἠθελησα)	I am willing, wish (w. infin.); I refuse; 'I will that...', followed by subj., ± ἱνα. I wish, desire (tr.)
θεμελιος	foundation (stone) [*theme*]
θεμελιοω	I found
θεος	God (± article); a god, deity [*theophany*]

195

θεραπευω	(I *serve*) I treat, heal, cure [*therapeutic*]
θεριζω	I reap
θερισμος	harvest
θεωρεω	I look at, gaze; I see, perceive [*theory, theorem*]
θησαυριζω	I treasure up
θησαυρος	a store, treasure [*thesaurus*]
θλιψις, -εως, ἡ	distress, trouble
θυγατηρ, -τρος	daughter
θυρα	door [indir., *thyroid gland*]
θυσια	sacrifice, offering
θυσιαστηριον	altar
θυω	I sacrifice, kill

I

ἰαομαι (1 aor. ἰασαμην)	I heal (physical and spiritual) [*psychiatry*]
ἰδε	see! behold! look! (imper. used as interjection)
ἰδιος, -α, -ον	one's own, private, personal [*idiom; idiot*]
ἰδου	see! behold! look! (strictly a demon. particle, w. wider use and more common than ἰδε)

ἱερευς, -εως a priest [*hierarchy*]

ἱερον temple (either whole building or outer courts – see **ναος**)

ἱκανος, -η, -ον considerable, sufficient; worthy, suitable

ἱματιον outer garment, cloak; (pl.) clothing

ἱνα (conj., mostly w. subj.) in order that…, so that… (It has six distinct uses, indicating: purpose, command, wish, consequence, noun-clause-introduction, and interrogative)
ἱνα μη that… not, lest

ἱστημι, στησω,
ἑστησα (and ἐστην),
ἑστηκα, ἑσταμαι,
ἐσταθην (tr.) in pres., imp., fut., 1 aor. act. and in pass. I make to stand, establish, set up;
(ἐστησα)

(intr.) in perf., plup. (w. sense of pres. and imp.) and in 2 aor. act. (ἐστην) I am set up, I stand

(There are a score of compounds for this important verb.)

ἰσχυρος, -α, -ον strong, powerful

ἰσχυω I have strength, prevail; I am able, I can (w. infin.) (cf. δυναμαι)

K

κἀγω (και ἐγω)	and I, even I, I also
καθαριζω	I cleanse, make clean (physically, ethically, ceremonially)
καθαρος, -α, -ον	clean, pure (as above) [*Katharine; cathartic*]
καθημαι	I am seated, I sit
καθιζω (intr.)	I sit (down), am seated; [cf. *cathedral*]
(rarely tr.)	I seat; I appoint
καθιστημι (see ἰστημι)	
(tr. tenses)	I set, establish, appoint
καθως	even as..., just as..., according as...
και	and, also; even
καινος, -η, -ον	new, fresh, novel (new w. regard to quality, see νεος)
καιρος	time, season (definite period or implying suitability – it has been suggested that it often means 'God's time', while χρονος refers to man's)
καιω	I ignite, I burn [*caustic*]
κατακαιω	I burn down
κἀκεινος, -η, -ο	(και ἐκεινος) and he, and she, and it; he, she, it also
κακια	wickedness, malice
κακος, -η, -ον	bad, evil [*cacophony*]

198

κακως	badly, evilly, ill
καλεω	I call, summon, invite; I call, name
καλος, -η, -ον	good (and seen to be so, cf. ἀγαθος); good, practically and ethically [*kaleidoscope; calligraphy*]
καλως	well, rightly, honourably
κἀν (και ἀν)	and if, even if, at least
καρδια	the heart; (the centre of all physical and spiritual life, hence:) mind, intellect, emotional state, will [*cardiac*]
καρπος	fruit; (fig.) action, result; profit, advantage [*Polycarp*]
κατα (prep. w. gen.)	against, down from, throughout; [*catastrophe*]
(w. acc.)	*(far more frequently w. acc. and w. numerous meanings)*: throughout, towards, over against (motion); at, in, by, of (adv. phrases); at, during, about (time); of place, time, numbers (distributively); concerning, according to (conformity)
καταβαινω, -βησομαι, -εβην, -βεβηκα	I go/come down, I descend (persons or things)
κατακρινω	I condemn, give judgement against
καταλαμβανω (see λαμβανω)	I lay hold of, seize; I overtake; (mid.) I comprehend
καταλειπω	I leave behind; I desert, abandon

καταλυω	(I loosen thoroughly) I break up, destroy (lit. and fig.)
καταργεω	(I make idle) I annul, abolish
κατεχω	I hold fast, possess; I hold back, restrain
κατηγορεω	I accuse, charge [*category*] (before a judge or in general)
κατοικεω (tr.) (intr.)	I inhabit, live in; I settle, dwell (Acts and Revelation)
καυχαομαι	I boast, 'glory in', exult
καυχημα, -ατος, το	boasting, 'glorying', exultation (grounds)
καυχησις, -εως, ἡ	boasting, 'glorying', exultation (act)
κειμαι	I have been placed; I lie (perf. used as pass. of τιθημι) (of persons, things, and fig.)
κενος, -η, -ον	empty; vain, fruitless [*cenotaph*; *kenotic doctrine*]
κεφαλη	the head (lit. and fig.) [*encephalitis; cephalopod*]
κηρυσσω	(I am a herald) I proclaim, preach
κλαιω	I weep, lament (for)
κλεπτης	a thief [*kleptomania*]
κλεπτω	I steal
κληρονομεω	I inherit, possess by inheritance
κληρονομια	inheritance, heritage

κληρονομος	an heir, inheritor
κλησις, -εως, ἡ	a calling, invitation
κλητος, -η, -ον	called, invited (both always of God in the New Testament)
κοιλια	belly, womb (general term covering any organ in the abdomen) [*coeliac*]
κοιμαομαι	I fall asleep, I am asleep (fig. of death) [*cemetery*]
κοινος, -η, -ον	common, shared; (Heb.) profane, unclean
κοινοω	I make unclean, profane
κοινωνεω	I share in, have fellowship with (mostly w. dat)
κοινωνος	a sharer, a partner (adj. used as noun)
κοινωνια	partnership, fellowship, communion; contribution
κομιζομαι	(mid.) I receive (back), recover
κοπιαω	I grow weary; I labour, toil (mental or physical effort)
κοπος	(weary) toil, labour; trouble
κοσμος	the universe; the (inhabited) world or earth; its human inhabitants; worldly affairs or possessions; the ungodly ('the world' as apart from God) [*cosmic; cosmetics*]
κραζω	I cry aloud, shriek, shout out
κρατεω	(I am powerful) I take hold of, obtain; I hold fast (fig.)

κρατος, -ους, το	power, might; dominion, rule [*democratic*]
κριμα, -ατος, το	a judgement, a verdict; condemnation
κρινω	I decide, determine; I judge (privately or in a law court); I condemn
κρισις, -εως, ἡ	decision, judgement (generally Divine) [*crisis*]
κριτης	a judge [*critic*]
κρυπτος, -η, -ον	hidden, secret [*cryptic, crypt*]
κρυπτω	I hide, conceal
κτιζω	I create, found, make (of God)
κτισις, -εως, ἡ	creating, creation (almost always of God), creature
Κυριος	owner, lord, master (of slaves or property); Sir! Sirs! Gentlemen! (vocative of polite address); Lord (of Divine Beings – God and gods). It is found ± the definite article when it refers to God the Father. However, when it alludes to the Christ, it tends to have the article, ὁ Κυριος.
κωλυω	I prevent, hinder (w. infin.: 'from…')
κωμη	a village, small town

Λ

λαλεω	I speak, say (more dignified than classical 'chatter') [cf. *glossolalia*]
λαμβανω, λημψομαι, ἐλαβον, εἰληφα, εἰλημμαι, ἐλημφθην	I take, lay hold of; I receive, get (*epilepsy*)
λαος	a people; the crowd [*laity*]
λατρευω	I serve, worship [*idolatry*]
λεγω, ἐρω, εἰπον, εἰρηκα, εἰρημαι, ἐρρηθην	I say, speak (incl. thought and writing). There are numerous other meanings for this 'defective' verb, according to context, such as: I assert, teach, command, mean, name, mention.
λιαν	very, exceedingly
λιθαζω, λιθοβολεω	I stone
λιθος	a stone [*Palaeolithic; offset-litho*]
λογιζομαι	I reckon up, count; I consider, suppose
λογος	(among a number of meanings) a word; a saying; speech, discourse; subject-matter, teaching; the Divine Word. The Logos – a Palestinian and/or Alexandrian conception, christianised by the Fourth Evangelist by identifying it with Jesus Christ. [*logic; philology*]

λοιπος, -η, -ον	(left behind) the remaining, the rest, the others
το λοιπον (adv. phrase)	for the future; for the rest, besides
λυπεω	I distress, grieve
λυπη	pain (body or mind), grief, sorrow
λυω	I unloose, release; (fig.) I break up, destroy [*analysis*]

M

μαθητης	learner, disciple [*mathematics*]
μακαριος, -α, -ον	happy, blessed [Archbishop *Makarios*]
μακραν	at a distance, far away
(advs.)	
μακροθεν	from a distance, from afar
μακροθυμεω	I am long-tempered
μακροθυμια	patience, long-suffering
μαλιστα	(superl. of unused μαλα) most of all, especially
μαλλον	(compar. of unused μαλα) (the) more, rather
μανθανω (2 aor. ἐμαθον)	I learn [*mathematics*]
μαρτυρεω	I witness, give evidence, testify
μαρτυριον, το, and μαρτυρια, ἡ	witness, evidence, testimony

μαρτυς, -υρος	a witness; a martyr
μαχαιρα	a (short) sword
μεγας, μεγαλη, μεγα	large, great (in widest sense) [*megaphone; omega*]
μειζων, -ονος, μειζον	(n.) (comp. of μεγας) greater, bigger
μελλω (w. infin.)	I am about to…, I intend… (free will or necessity); (abs. in pres. part.) coming, future (dist. from μελει impers. w. dat.: it is a care to)
μεν	a generally untranslatable particle (occurring some one hundred and eighty times), answered by δε or other conj., each of the two introducing a clause to be contrasted with the other, e.g., 'I indeed… but He…' (Matt. 3:11). The μεν is very often omitted as compared w. classical Greek.
μενω (1 aor. ἐμεινα)	I remain, stay (numerous compounds) [cf. *permanent*]
μεριμνα	care, worry, anxiety
μεριμναω	I am anxious; I care for
μερος, -ους, το	a share, portion; a part [*polymer*]
adv. phrases:	
ἀπο, ἐκ μερους	in part, partly;
ἀνα, κατα μερος	part-by-part, in detail
μεσος, -η, -ον	middle, in the middle [*Mesopotamia*]

μετα (prep. w. gen.)	with, in company with (more common than συν);
(w. acc.)	after (almost always of time); compounded w. vbs., it means association, exchange or 'after'. [*Metaphysics*]
μεταβαινω (2 aor. μετεβην)	I pass over; I withdraw, leave
μετανοεω	I change mind, I repent
μετανοια	change of mind, repentance
μεχρι (prep. w. gen.)	as far as, until, even to (chiefly of time);
(rare as conj.)	until
μη (negative particle)	Not (Used where something is indefinite or hypothetical, as opposed to ού the negative of fact. Normally ού negates the indicative; μη, the other moods – usually including participles.)
adv.	Not, w. subj., infin., partic., imper., opt.
conj.	after vbs. of fearing, caution etc.
interrog.	for hesitant questions or those expecting answer 'No'.
ού μη	w. aor. subj. or fut. indic. for emphatic negation: assuredly not, by no means. (See ού)
μηδε	(generally after preceding μη)
(conj.)	but not, and not, neither/ nor;
(adv.)	not even

μηδεις, μηδεμια, μηδεν	(adj.) no, none; (noun) (m. and f.) no person, nobody, (n.) nothing (related to οὐδεις as μη to οὐ)
μηκετι	no longer (used in same constructions as μη)
μην, -ος, ὁ	month [*menopause*]
μηποτε	lest ever, lest perhaps
μητε	neither, nor
μητε... μητε	neither... nor
μητηρ, -ρος, ἡ	mother [*metropolis*; cf. *maternal*]
μητι	interrog. particle expecting neg. answer and used in hesitant questions
μια	(fem. of εἱς) one
μικρος, -α, -ον	small, little [*microscope*; *omicron*]
ἐλαχιστος, -η, -ον	smallest, least
μιμνησκομαι	(lit. I remind myself) I remember (w. gen.)
μισεω	I hate [*misogynist*]
μισθος	pay, wages; reward, recompense
μνημειον and μνημα, -ατος, το	monument, tomb
μνημονευω	I remember [*mnemonic*]
μοιχευω	I commit adultery
μοιχεια	adultery
μοιχος	adulterer

μοιχαλις, -ιδος, ἡ	adulteress; disloyal (adj.)
μονον (adv.)	alone, only
μονος, -η, -ον (adj.)	alone, only [*monotheism*]
μυστηριον	a secret, mystery

N

ναι	yes
ναος	a temple; an inner shrine (see ἱερον)
νεκρος, -α, -ον (adj.) (as noun)	dead, lifeless (lit. and fig.); the dead, a corpse [*necropolis*]
νεος, -α, -ον	new (properly re time – see καινος); young [*neolithic*]
νοεω, κατανοεω	I understand, perceive; I think, consider
νομος	law, ordinance; the Mosaic Law [*economy*]
νους, νοος, ὁ	mind, reason, intellect [slang '*nous*']
νυν, νυνι	now (sometimes with a prep.); the present (w. article)
νυξ, νυκτος, ἡ	night

Ξ

No words

Ο

ὁ, ἡ, το (m., f., n.)	definite article, 'the';
distributive use, e.g.:	
ὁ μεν... ὁ δε	the one... the other;
in narration:	ὁ δε, but he
	It is found w. nouns and names (and w. nom. instead of voc.), adjectives, participles, infinitives, adverbs, numerals, prepositional and other phrases such as quotations, and w. nouns in genitive to denote kinship. The gen. s. n. του w. infin. is used in three special ways (like ἱνα): purpose, consequence, and introducing a noun clause.
ὁδος, ἡ	a road, way; a journey; (hence fig.) a way of life, course of conduct [*method; hodometer*]
οἰδα	(from same root as εἰδον) I know (a fact);
(w. infin.)	I know how to...; I know (a person)
οἰκια	a house, (occasionally) household (also fig. usages)
οἰκοδομεω	I build (a house); hence fig.

οἶκος	a house (legally included whole estate); household, family [*economy; diocese*]
οἰκουμενη	(γη understood) the inhabited world (originally by Greeks; later the Roman world; in the New Testament also of the whole inhabited earth) [*ecumenical*]
οἶνος	wine
ὀλιγος, -η, -ον	(in pl.) few; (in s.) small, short, slight [*oligarchy*]
ὁλος, -η, -ον	whole, all [*holocaust*]
ὀμνυμι, ὀμνυω (1 aor. ὠμοσα)	I swear, take an oath
ὁμοιος, -α, -ον	like, similar [*homoiousian; homoeopathy*]
ὁμοιοω	I make like, compare
ὁμοιως	similarly, likewise
ὁμολογεω	(orig. to speak same language/agree with) I confess, admit, declare; also ἐξομολογουμαι with similar meanings
ὀνειδιζω	I reproach
ὀνειδισμος	a reproach, rebuke
ὀνομα, -ατος, το	a name; (in Heb. and Hellenistic usage) personality, authority of the owner [*onomatopoeia*]
ὀπισω (adv.) (prep. w. gen.)	behind, after (place) behind, after (place and time)

ὅπου	where; to where; indefinite construction ὅπου ἄν wheresoever, whithersoever
ὅπως	in order that (purpose clause w. subj. ± ἄν); that (after verbs of asking, encouraging etc.) It is much rarer than ἵνα
ὁράω (in prohibitions)	I see; I perceive, discern; see... do not, beware lest... (a 'defective verb', in which other tenses are supplied by different roots: ὄψομαι, εἶδον, ἑώρακα, —, ὤφθην) [panorama]
ὀργή	anger; wrath (of God) (momentary or permanent state)
ὄρος, -ους, το	a mountain
ὅς, ἥ, ὅ	who (whom), which, what, that (definite relative pron., agreeing in gender and number w. its antecedent) (it is also used as demonstrative pron.: this, that; the one... the other)
ὅσος, -η, -ον	(Lat. quantus) how much/many; how great; how far/ long (of quantity, degree, space and time)
ὅστις, ἥτις, ὅ τι (a)	(ὅς and τις both declined, as with 'Respublica', but it is almost always nominative) of indefinite person or thing, ± ἄν (ἐαν) and subj.: whoever, anyone who; whichever, anything which

(b)		of definitive person or thing regarding quality:
		(i) generic 'who/which, as other like things'; or
		(ii) essential 'who/which, by its very nature'.
(c)		where the relative sentence expresses a reason or consequence
(d)		occasionally similar to simple ὅς

ὅταν — whenever (re indefinite fut., w. subj.); when (w. indic.)

ὅτε — when (w. indic.)

ὅτι — because; that (introducing noun clauses after vbs. of saying, thinking, knowing, seeing, feeling)

οὗ (relative adv.) — where; (sometimes) where to, whither

οὐ (negative particle) — (οὐκ before smooth breathings; οὐχ before rough) not

οὐ (interjection) — No!
It is generally employed w. indic. and for a denial of fact (see μη). In questions, it expects the answer 'Yes'.
[*Utopia* – *'no place'*]

οὐδε (conj.) — and not, neither, nor
(adv.) — not even

οὐδεις, οὐδεμια, οὐδεν (noun) no one, nothing; (adj.) no

οὐδεποτε — never

οὐκετι — no longer, no more

οὖν	so, therefore, then (conj., never first in a sentence)
οὔπω	not yet
οὐρανος	the sky; heaven (pl. sometimes used, owing to conception of at least three heavens) [*Uranus*]
οὖς, ὤτος, το	ear [*otology*]
οὔτε	and not, neither, nor;
οὔτε... οὔτε	neither... nor
οὖτος, αὐτη, τουτο	this; he, she, it, they (demon. adj. and pron.)
οὔτως (sic)	so, thus, in this way
οὐχι	not at all, not so (a more emphatic form of οὐ, not); used in questions expecting the answer 'Yes'.
ὀφειλω	I owe; (w. infin.) I ought to... (disting. from ὠφελεω I help)
ὀφθαλμος	eye [*ophthalmic*]
ὀχλος	crowd, throng; common people, mob [*ochlocracy – mob rule*]
ὀψια	early evening, twilight, dusk

Π

παθημα, -ατος, το	(an experience – see πασχω) suffering [*apathy; pathology*]
παιδευω	I instruct, educate; I chastise

παιδιον	little boy, child; (also of older children and of adults affectionately)
παις, παιδος	child (boy or girl); male slave, servant [*pedagogue; orthopaedic*]
παλιν (adv.)	again; moreover [*palindrome; palimpsest*]
παντοτε (adv.)	always
παρα	basic meaning 'beside'
(prep. w. acc.)	by, beside, along (w. vbs. of motion and rest, properly of place); against, contrary to (opp. of κατα); [*paradox*] more than, above (in comparisons);
(w. gen.)	from side of, from beside (chiefly w. persons – relations, companions, possessions);
(w. dat.)	by, beside [*paragraph*](almost always w. persons); among, in house of ('chez'); in eyes/judgement of (all three uses are of similar frequency and distribution)
παραβολη	comparison; parable
παραγγελλω	I command, charge
παραγινομαι	I come near, I arrive at (Lucan)
παραδιδωμι	(see διδωμι) I hand over; I deliver up, betray; I hand down
παρακαλεω	I entreat, beg; I exhort, admonish; I comfort, encourage
παρακλησις, -εως, ἡ	exhortation; consolation [*Paraclete*]

παραλαμβανω	(see λαμβανω) I receive from; I take to/with me
παραπτωμα, -ατος, το	(a falling-beside) lapse, trespass
παρατιθημι	(see τιθημι) I place beside, I serve;
(mid.)	I deposit with, I entrust to
παρειμι (see εἰμι)	I am present, at hand (mostly of persons); I have come, arrived
παρερχομαι	(see ἐρχομαι) I pass by, I pass (persons and things);
(fig.)	I pass away, perish
παρεχω (act. and mid.)	I show, cause (w. immaterial things); I present, supply
παριστημι	(see ἱστημι)

tr. tenses (pres., fut., imp., 1 aor.):   I place beside, present, provide;

intr. tenses (perf., 2 aor., plup.):   I stand by, beside; I appear; I am present

παρουσια	presence; (mostly) arrival, advent (technical term for visitation of a king or official) [*Parousia*]
παρρησια	free speech (παρρησια adv. openly, plainly); confidence, boldness

πας, πασα, παν (παντος gen., m. and n.)
        (adj.)   (s.) every; the whole, all the...
                  (pl.) all; all the...
    (as pron.) everyone, everything; all, all things
                  [*Panorama*]

πασχα	(only article το declines) Passover feast, paschal meal
πασχω (2 aor. ἐπαθον)	(originally 'neutral': I am acted on, I experience – Acts 9:16.; Gal. 3:4 in good sense)
	I experience ill treatment, I suffer [*pathology*]
πατηρ, πατρος	father; male ancestor; God the Father. (Attributes are sometimes placed w. the divine meaning. In addition, 'father' can be a courtesy title and there are various figurative uses.) [cf. *paternal*]
παυω (mid., intr.)	I cease; [*pause*]
(act. tr., rare)	I stop
πειθω, πεισω, ἐπεισα, πεποιθα, πεπεισμαι, ἐπεισθην	
(tr.)	I urge, I try to persuade;
(intr.)	I trust, I am confident;
(mid. or pass.)	I am persuaded, I believe; I obey (w. dat.)
πειναω	I hunger (lit. and fig.)
πειραζω	I try, test, make trial of (God to man; and vice-versa in another sense); I tempt; I try, attempt (w. infin.) [*empirical; pirate*]
πειρασμος	trial, probation, testing; temptation
πεμπω, πεμψω, ἐπεμψα, —, πεμπομαι, ἐπεμφθην	I send [*pomp*]
πεντε, οἱ, αἱ, τα	five [*Pentateuch; pentagon*]

περαν (prep. w. gen.)	beyond, across
το περαν	the other side, the country beyond
περι (prep. mainly w. gen.)	concerning, about; with regard to, on account of;
(w. acc. local and occasionally temporal)	around, about [*perimeter* re space; *perinatal* re time]
περιπατεω	I walk; I conduct life, live [*peripatetic*]
περισσευω　(intr.) 　　　　　　(tr.)	I overflow, abound; I excel; I cause to exceed
περισσος, -η, -ον	exceeding, excessive; uncommon, superior
περισσοτερως	(comp. adv.) more exceedingly, more abundantly
περιτεμνω	I cut around, circumcise
περιτομη	circumcision (the rite, the state, meton. and fig.)
πινω (2 aor. ἐπιον)	I drink
πιπτω (2 aor. ἐπεσον)	I fall (of descent – persons and things – homage etc.)
πιστευω　(intr.)	I believe, have faith (abs. or w. dat.); I believe, trust in/on (followed by εἰς, ἐπι w. acc. or ἐν, ἐπι w. dat.)
(rarely tr.)	I entrust
πιστις, -εως, ἡ	(almost always in active sense) faith, belief, trust; the (*Christian*) Faith

πιστος, -η, -ον (pass.) trusty, faithful; reliable, sure;
(act.) believing, trusting, relying

πλαναω (mostly fig.)
(act.) I lead astray, deceive;
(pass.) I am led astray, err [*planet* – from lit. sense 'to wander']

πλανη a wandering, error

πλανος, -ον deceiving; a deceiver

πλειων, πλειον (comp. of πολυς)
(adj.) more; larger;
(noun) the greater number, the more [*pleonasm*]

πλην (conj.) however, nevertheless;
(prep. w. gen.) except, apart from (similar to χωρις, but rare in this sense)

πληροω I fulfil, complete, accomplish (duties or prophecies)

πληρης, -ες full (sometimes not declined)

πληρωμα, -ατος, το (mainly in passive sense) fullness, complement

πλοιον a boat, a ship (ναυς ship – once only)

πλουσιος, -α, -ον rich, wealthy (more often material)

πλουτος, ὁ and το riches, wealth (material or spiritual) [*plutocrat*]

πνευμα, -ατος, το In the New Testament there are five distinct usages. Recourse should be made to a lexicon, but in brief:

	(1) wind, breath (from πνεω I blow)
	(2) the spirit (as opposed to body, flesh etc.)
	(3) spirit (frame of mind, disposition)
	(4) a spirit (mostly, but not always, evil)
	(5) the Holy Spirit (normally w. article when regarded as a Person; without, when reference is to operation, influence, or gift.)

In the Greek LXX or Septuagint, of the 3rd century BC, πνευμα translates the Hebrew 'ruach', wind, the invading Spirit of Yahweh; ψυχη translates 'nephesh', breath, the personal soul. [*pneumatic*]

πνευματικος, -η, -ον	(πνευμα characteristics) spiritual (persons and things)
ποθεν;	where from? whence? (place, origin, cause)
ποιεω	I make, produce; I do, perform [*poet; pharmacopoeia*]
ποιμαινω	I shepherd, tend
ποιμην, -ενος	shepherd
ποιμνη (also -ιον)	flock
ποιος, -α, -ον;	what sort of? what? (dir. and indir. questions)
πολις, -εως, ἡ	a city (sometimes referring to citizens) [*political; Neapolis*]
πολλακις (adv.)	often, frequently
πολυς, πολλη, πολυ	much, many; (of time) long;

(as pl. noun)	many persons;
(n. pl. as adv.)	πολλα much (note – one λ when followed by 'υ') [*polytheism*]
πονηρος, -α, -ον	bad, evil, wicked (persons or things);
ὁ πονηρος	evil one, Satan, the Devil;
το πονηρον	the evil in the world, all that is wicked
πορευομαι	I journey, proceed, go (also fig.)
(εἰσπορευομαι	I go in; ἐκπορευομαι I go out)
πορνεια	fornication
πορνη	prostitute
πορνος	fornicator, male prostitute [*pornography*]
ποσος, -η, -ον	how much(?) how many(?) how great(?) (dir. and indir. questions)
ποτε (indef. temp. particle)	once, formerly, sometime
ποτε; (interrog. adv.)	when? (w. ἑως how long?)
ποτηριον	cup (lit. and fig.)
ποτιζω	I cause to drink [cf. *potion*]
που;	where?; (= ὁπου) where (w. indic. or subj.); where to? whither? (dir. and indir. questions)
πους, ποδος, ὁ	foot [*podium; chiropodist*]
πραγμα, -ατος, το	deed, action (past); [*pragmatic*] matter, affair (present)

πραξις, -εως, ἡ	doing, action
πρασσω	I accomplish, perform, do (Lucan and Pauline) [*practical*]
πραΰς, -εια, -υ	gentle, meek
πραΰτης, -ητος, ἡ	gentleness, meekness
πρεσβυτερος, -α, -ον (of age)	(strictly a compar. adj.) the elder of two, old, aged; ancestors;
(as Jewish title of honour) (among Christians)	member of Sanhedrin, an 'elder'; an 'elder' or 'presbyter' of congregation or church;
(in Apocalypse)	one of the twenty-four elders. (In the New Testament it appears to be synonymous w. ἐπισκοπος, and can be called for convenience presbyter-bishop.)
προ	(prep. w. gen., mainly time, but also of place) before, earlier than; before, in front of; [*prologue*] it is sometimes found w. article in genitive and the infinitive; joined w. other words, it can mean priority, intensity, preference.
προαγω	I precede, go before; I lead forward
προβατον	a sheep
προλεγω (see λεγω)	I tell/ say beforehand; I declare plainly
προς (prep. w. acc.)	to, towards (of persons, places, things; w. vbs. of motion and saying).

Some other senses: near; with (hostile or friendly relations) [*proselyte*]; for (indicating purpose or result); according to, with regard to.

προς w. gen. and dat. both very rare

προσδεχομαι	I receive, accept; I await, expect
προσδοκαω	I expect, wait for
προσερχομαι	(see ἐρχομαι) I come to, I approach
προσευχη	prayer
προσευχομαι	I pray (followed by a dozen different prepositions, cases etc.)
προσεχω	I attend to, turn mind to (understand τον νουν); I attend to myself; I join, devote myself to
προσκαλεομαι	I call to myself
προσκυνεω	(usually w. dat.) I worship, do obeisance to
προστιθημι	(see τιθημι) I place/put to, I add, join to [*prosthesis* – grammar and surgery]
προσφερω	(see φερω) I bring to, lead to; I offer (sacrifices etc.)
προσωπον	human face; look, countenance; presence (esp. when applied to God); outward appearance (of people and things).

	(Because of the Hebraistic idiom, 'face' is sometimes redundant.)
προτερον	(adv. acc. of obsolescent compar. προτερος) formerly, previously
προφητεια	declaration, 'prophecy' (Old Testament and New Testament. Not necessarily re future)
προφητευω	I declare God's will (not necessarily prediction), I prophesy
προφητης, -ου	a prophet – one who *tells forth*, declares in speech, the will of God regarding past, present, or future. It includes ones in the Old Testament, prophets in general, John the Baptist, Christ Himself, Christian prophets, and prophetic writings.
πρωϊ (adv.)	early
πρωϊα, ἡ (adj. used as noun)	early morning
πρωτον (adv.)	first, at the first (mostly of time; occasionally of order)
πρωτος, -η, -ον	(superlative, but doing duty also for obsolescent comparative προτερος) first (time or place, as noun or adj.); chief, principal (status) [*prototype; Proto-Luke*]
πτωχος, -η, -ον	poor; (as noun) a beggar (also fig.)
πυρ, πυρος, το	fire (lit. and fig., and eschatologically of Gehenna) [*pyre; pyrotechnics*]

πωλεω (and πιπρασκω) I sell [*monopoly*]

πως;   how? (in direct questions); how (in indirect);
how! (in exclamations)

πως   (indef. enclitic – much less frequent than πως; above) in some/any way, at all; μηπως lest perhaps

P

ρημα, -ατος, το   spoken word, utterance (concrete expression of λογος);

(pl.)   speech, discourse;
a saying, word of prophecy [cf. *rhetoric*]

Σ

σαββατον
and   the Sabbath (approx. 6 p.m. Fri. - Sat.); a week

σαββατα (pl.)   (two reasons for this plural form: it was transliterated from Aramaic 'shabbata' and mistakenly made into a singular; two or three festivals have, in fact, plural endings)

σαρξ, σαρκος, ἡ   flesh; body (as a whole); (idiomatic usage, e. g.) physical nature, human frailty [*sarcasm; sarcophagus*]

σεαυτον, -ου, -ῳ	(2nd pers. sing. reflexive pron.) yourself, of, to yourself (only m. used in N.T.)
σημειον	a sign (distinguishing, warning, or predicting); a miracle, wonder [*semantic; semaphore*]
σημερον	today
σκανδαλιζω	(lit. I ensnare, cause to stumble) I repel, offend
σκανδαλον	stumbling-block, cause of offence [*scandal*]
σκευος, -ους, το	a vessel, implement; τα σκευη utensils, property; (fig. of people)
σκοτος, -ους, το	and ἡ σκοτια darkness [*scotoscope*] (fig. of moral and spiritual darkness)
σος, ση, σον	your (2nd pers. sing.), thy, thine
σοφια	wisdom (divine and human) [*philosophy;* cf. *sophomore*]
σπειρω	I sow (lit. and fig.)
σπερμα, -ατος, το	seed; offspring, descendants [*sperm*]
σπλαγχνιζομαι	I feel sorry for
σπλαγχνα (n. pl.)	(inward parts) compassion, pity
σπουδαζω	I hasten; I am eager
σπουδη	haste; eagerness
σταυρος	a cross, the Crucifixion
σταυροω	I crucify

στηριζω	I confirm, strengthen
στομα, -ατος, το	the mouth [*St. Chrysostom* -'*golden-mouth'; colostomy*]
στρατευμα, -ατος, το	an army
στρατευομαι	I serve in the army, make war [*strategy*]
στρατιωτης	a soldier
στρεφω	I turn; (pass. reflexive) I turn myself [*strophe*]
συ, σε, σου, σοι	(2nd pers. sing. declined) you/thou (the nom. for emphasis or contrast), you (acc.), of you, to/for you
συμφερω	(intrans. and generally impersonal – συμφερει) it is an advantage, expedient (as partic.: profitable; profit)
συν (prep. w. dat.)	with, in company with [*syntax; synthetic*] (chiefly Luke, Acts, and Paul – about half as frequent as μετα meaning 'with')
συναγω	I gather together, collect [*synagogue*]
συναγωγη	(religious) assembly, a synagogue (either congregation or building)
συνεδριον	the Council of seventy-one members at Jerusalem; a local Jewish tribunal
συνειδησις, -εως, ἡ	conscience
συνερχομαι	I come together, assemble;

(2 aor. – ηλθον)	I accompany
συνιημι (1 aor. συνηκα)	I understand, perceive
σχιζω	I tear, split, divide
σχισμα, -ατος, το	a tear, split, division [*schism; schizophrenia*]
σωζω	I save, rescue (from danger, illness, or sin)
σωμα, -ατος, το	the body (alive or dead) – physical nature as against πνευμα or ψυχη. Fig. of the Church as the Body of Christ [*psychosomatic*]
σωτηρ, -ηρος, ὁ	saviour, deliverer, preserver (used of God and His Son)
σωτηρια	salvation, deliverance (sacred and secular) [*soteriology*]

T

ταπεινος, -η, -ον	low degree, humble
ταπεινοφροσυνη	humility
ταπεινοω	I humble, make low
ταρασσω	I trouble, perplex
ταχεως, ταχυ	quickly, speedily, hastily [*tachycardia*]
τε	and (copulative particle, similar to Latin -*que*, denoting a closer connection than the conj. και. Frequent in Acts.)

τε... και, τε και, τε... τε	both... and
τεκνον	child (also used in affection to adults); also fig. 'child of wisdom'
τελειος, -α, -ον	complete, perfect (persons and things)
τελειοω	I complete, perfect
τελεω	I end, finish; I fulfil
τελος, -ους, το	end, result, fulfilment [*teleology*]
τερας, -ατος, το	wonder, marvel
τηρεω	I guard, preserve; I observe, obey (of regulations) [cf. φυλασσω]
τιθημι, θησω, ἐθηκα, τεθεικα, τεθειμαι, ἐτεθην	I put, place, set forth; I appoint [*antithesis; synthetic*]
τιμη	honour; price [*Timothy*]
τις; (m. and f.), τι; (n.), τινος; interrog. pron. and adj.: who? which? what?; why?	
τις (m. and f.), τι (n.) τινος	(indefinite pron. and adj.): one, a certain one, some; someone, anyone, something, anything; (adj.) a certain, some The stem in both cases is τιν-, and follows third declension endings.
τοιουτος, -αυτη, -ουτο(ν)	of such a kind, such

τολμαω (usually w. infin.) I dare, have courage, venture (to…)

τοπος   place [*topography; topic*]

τοσουτος, -αυτη, -ουτο(ν)   so great; so much, (pl.) so many

τοτε   (Matthaean favourite) then, at that time; thereupon

τραπεζα   a table [*trapezium; trapeze*]

τρεις, τρια (n.)   three [*triad*]

τρεχω (2 aor. ἐδραμον)   I run (the vb. has eight compounds) [cf. *syndrome; dromedary*]

τριτος, -η, -ον   third (τριτον adv. acc. – thirdly) [*Trito-Isaiah*]

τροπος   manner, way [*tropic*]

τροφη   nourishment, food

τρεφω   I nourish, feed [*atrophy*]

τυγχανω (2 aor. ἐτυχον)   (w. gen.) I obtain, reach; (abs.) I chance, happen

τυπος   figure, image; pattern, model [*type*]

τυπτω   I strike, beat [cf. *tympanum, timpani*]

τυφλος, -η, -ον   blind (lit. and fig.)

Υ

ὑγιαινω   I am well, sound (lit. and fig.)

ὑγιης, -ες	healthy, sound [*hygiene*]
ὑδωρ, ὑδατος, το	water [*hydrant; hydrangea*]
υἱος	son (lit. and fig.)
ὑμεις, ὑμας, ὑμων, ὑμιν	you (pl. declined of συ 'thou'; nom. for emphasis or contrast)
ὑμετερος, -α, -ον	your, yours
(ἡμετερος, -α, -ον	our, ours)
ὑπαγω	I go away slowly, withdraw, depart
ὑπακοη	obedience
ὑπακουω	(I hearken to) I obey
ὑπαρχω	I am (a permanent state, rather than a temporary or accidental one); I belong to (Lucan favourite)
τα ὑπαρχοντα	one's possessions, property
ὑπερ (prep. w. gen.) (w. acc.) (less common)	for, on behalf of; for sake of; over, beyond (indicating excess) [*hypercritical*]
ὑπηρετης	servant, attendant, minister, officer (acc. to context)
ὑπο (prep.)	(before smooth breathing ὑπ', before rough breathing ὑφ')
w. gen.	by (direct agent)
w. acc.	under (lit. and fig. after verbs of motion and rest) [*hypodermic*]
ὑπομενω	I bear patiently, endure
ὑπομονη	patience, endurance

ὑποστρεφω	I turn back, return (intr.) (Lucan favourite)
ὑποτασσω (act.) (mid. and pass.)	I subject; I submit
ὑστερεω	I am in want, come short (of)
ὑστερημα, -ατος, το	the lacking; poverty
ὑψηλος, -η, -ον	high
ὑψιστος, -η, -ον	highest
ὑψος, -ους, το	height
ὑψοω	I raise to height, exalt (usually fig.)

Φ

φαινω (act.) (pass.)	I give light, shine; I appear, become visible [*Epiphany; phantom*]
φανερος, -α, -ον	clear, visible, 'open'
φανεροω	I make clear, visible
φερω, οἰσω, ἠνεγκον, – ενηνοχα, —, ἠνεχθην (cf. Lat.: *fero, tuli, latum*)	I carry, bear; I bring (common defective verb, in which other tenses are supplied by different roots – cf. English 'go' and 'went'.) The verb has a dozen compounds. [*Christopher*]
φευγω (2 aor. ἐφυγον)	I flee; I escape [*fugitive*, via Latin]
φημι (2 aor. ἐφην)	I say (often in quoting or interjecting)
φιλεω	I love (of friendship) [*philanthropy*]

φιλος	a friend [*bibliophile*]
φοβεομαι	I fear; I reverence
φοβος	fear (sometimes reverential), terror [*phobia*]
φονευς, -εως	murderer
φονευω	I murder
φονος	murder
φρονεω	I think (of), am mindful of (serious interest, rather than casual opinion) [cf. *phrenology*]
φρονιμος, -ον	sensible, prudent
φυλακη	(a) guard; a prison; a watch of the night
φυλασσω	I guard, watch, protect; I keep, observe (customs and regulations)[*prophylactic*]
φωνεω	I cry out, shout; I call, summon
φωνη	a sound; a voice [*telephone; phonetics*]
φως, φωτος, το	light [*photography*]

X

χαιρω (2 aor. ἐχαρην w. act. meaning)	I rejoice, am glad; (imper. for salutations:) Hail! Greetings!
χαρα	joy, delight
χαριζομαι	I graciously give; I forgive

χαρις, -ιτος, ἡ (acc. χαριν)	grace, favour, charm; gratitude, thanks; also, in special Christian sense of freeness and universality of Divine grace and favour [*Charis, Charissa*]
χαρισμα, -ατος, το	a gracious gift, a spiritual endowment [*charismatic*]
χειρ, -ος, ἡ (dat. pl. χερσι)	hand [*chiropodist*]
χηρα	a widow
χρεια	need, necessity
χρονος	time; a period (in sense of duration; see καιρος for 'God's time') [*chronology*]
χρυσιον, χρυσος	gold (coin, ornaments) [*chrysanthemum; St. Chrysostom – golden mouth*]
χωλος, -η, -ον	lame
χωρα	land, region, (the) country
χωριον	piece of land, property
χωρις (prep. w. gen.)	apart from, without (see πλην as prep.)

Ψ

ψευδομαι	I lie
ψευδος, -ους, το	an untruth

ψευδ -   false – (ten words so compounded)
                [*pseudonym*]

ψυχη   life; soul; self [*psychology*]

Ω

ὡδε (adv.)   here (rest); 'hither' (motion)

ὡρα   an hour; time [*horology; horoscope*]

ὡς (adv.)   as (ὡς... οὑτως, or vice versa: as...
                so, so... as; w. nom., acc., prep., vb.,
                part. or gen. abs.);

                about (before numbers);

                how (before adjs. and advs.)

      (conj.)   temporal: as, when, since;
                while, when, as long as;

                final: in order that, to (w. infin.)

ὡσαυτως   similarly, likewise

ὡσει   as if, as it were; (w. numbers) about

ὡσπερ   just as, even as
                (περ, an enclitic particle, adds
                intensive force or positiveness to the
                word to which it is joined – indeed, by
                far)

ὡστε   1.   so that, so as to (w. infin. in
                consecutive clauses; negative μη);

234

2.	so then, consequently (w. a main clause in indic. or imper., with result stated merely as a new fact; negative οὐ)
ὠφελέω	I help, benefit [*Ophelia* – coined 1504?] (dist. from ὀφειλω I owe, ought)

Select Bibliography

Courses

Wenham, J.W., *The Elements of New Testament Greek*, Cambridge (Based on H.P.V. Nunn's earlier work, which has stood the test of time)

Beetham, Frank, *An Introduction to New Testament Greek*, Bristol Classical Press

Balaam, Alison and Beetham, Frank, *Tutor's Manual* for the above, Bristol Classical Press

Dobson, John H., *Learn New Testament Greek,* Bible Society

Morrice, William G., *The Durham New Testament Greek Course (2nd ed.)* (For 1st year Honours Theology)

Dictionaries

Souter, Alexander, *A Pocket Lexicon to the Greek New Testament,* Oxford (a useful *vade mecum*, but suffers from brevity)

Abbott-Smith, G., *A Manual Greek Lexicon of the New Testament* T & T Clark, (A good intermediate size work, with two invaluable appendices on verbs and giving Septuagint uses of Greek words and the Hebrew ones which they translate. It is not up to date.)

Bauer, Walter, *A Greek-English Lexicon of the New Testament (2nd ed.),* Chicago and London, (A scholarly tome, translated and augmented by Arndt & Gingrich)

Metzger, Bruce M., *Lexical Aids for Students of New Testament Greek (3rd ed.)*, T & T Clark 1969, (A pioneer work on word frequency, but is not concerned with distribution. It has useful classifications and a vivid diagram for prepositions.)

Commentary

Zerwick S.J., Max, and Grosvenor, Mary, *A Grammatical Analysis of The Greek New Testament* (5th revised edition), Rome, 1996